"Dr. Marjorie Barlow taps the pulse of enlightenment and empowerment in her newest book, *The Possible Woman Steps Up*. With both the practical and visionary insight, she leads the field in bringing harmony, power and creativity to women and their families throughout the world."

–Don Campbell, author of *Healing at the Speed of Sound*
and *The Mozart Effect*

"I have never met anyone who is a stronger advocate for women than Marj Barlow. Marj herself, personifies all that makes women so remarkable. Her compassion, strength, wisdom, humor, and intelligence are so obvious throughout this book. Marj has done much in her amazing career to promote inner peace, strength, and wellbeing for both genders. *The Possible Woman Steps Up* is a must-read for every woman who is looking for a happier and more successful 'you'. It is such an honor to call Marj Barlow both friend and mentor."

–John Wells, President and CEO Interface Americas

"Dr. Marjorie Barlow has DONE IT AGAIN! She has created a numinous and profound treatise about women as leaders - past, present and future; where women have evolved from, where they are today, and where they are headed to enlighten, inspire and lead the world we live in today. She is the Possible Woman® she describes so aptly in her new book; Servant Leader, Visionary, Creative Thinker, Feeler, Change Agent, Compassionate and Empathetic Mother, Caretaker of the Planet, Wise Old Woman, Friend, Companion and Heart Center. She is, above all, deeply committed to life-long learning, friends and family, sustainability, leaving a legacy and becoming the Possible Human. And she is, forevermore, The Possible Woman® at her very best!"

–Linda K. Wind. CEO, Wind Enterprises, and Creator,
Possible Woman® Leadership Conferences and Events

"The Possible Woman Steps Up is a beautiful journey that gently opens the door of awareness of who we are and more importantly, who we can become in our lives. Dr. Marj Barlow's wisdom not only allowed me to discover my full potential as a female leader in the corporate world, she gave me the gift of expanding my inner strength and courage to help other women discover their passion and purpose in life (through each chapter)."

–Amy Lukken, VP of Cultural Development, Joyologist, InterfaceFLOR

"The Possible Woman Steps Up is a book for woman and for men—a great read—great gift of Learning, teaching us how to explore what is possible. It describes our strategy for developing mind share and creating new relationships."

—Claude Ouimet InterfaceFLOR, Senior V.P. General Manager
for Canada and Latin America

"Marj Barlow is one of those rare individuals who deeply cares about people and helping them reach their full potential. "The Possible Woman Steps Up" is a compilation of Marj's proven frameworks and techniques for discovering your best self, growing your relationships, and remembering to have fun along the way. Treat this book like a workbook, working on one chapter at a time, to fully give yourself the time and space to explore and synthesize the themes. You'll end feeling empowered to tackle the world."

—Melissa Vernon, LEED AP, Director of Sustainable Strategy, InterfaceFLOR

"This book is exceptionally powerful. The material is so powerfully in-depth, is there a way to get it published for college curriculum, say Women's Studies programs? How fortunate young women are to have access to this thinking. And us older ones as well!"

—Cindi Marshall Oakey, Aware Consulting, Inc.

"Marj Barlow has transformed the lives of hundreds of women with her revolutionary vision, her exceptional wisdom, and her deep love. One always leaves her presence with a gift of laughter and inspiration for the next part of the journey.

She uses gentle humor and laser insight to lead women into their futures both as individuals and as the face of the rising culture.

Marj is an exceptional visionary, and an inspirational guide to inspire women everywhere into their callings.

With a delightful blend of personal story and specific activities, Marj Barlow reminds women everywhere of their importance to the future of our planet.

With compassion, humor, and fabulous advice, Marj Barlow reminds us that female leadership is essential to the future of the culture. Then, with great clarity and specificity she shows us how to get there."

—Cynthia Sullivan, Retired Teacher

"The Possible Woman Steps Up didn't come a minute too soon. When I start feeling anything less than good, I just open up the book, go to any page, and the words give me hope and energy. This book reminds me of what my mother (at her best) would say to me, 'Little girl, just remember who you are.'"

–Colleen Reeves, Red Corral Ranch
Wimberley, TX

"What an incredible gift to have Dr. Barlow's wisdom collected in one place. As a student of her insight for years, I encourage every woman to embrace this book as a highly relevant guide to achieving authentic success in today's world."

–Lindsay James, Director of Strategic Sustainability,
LEED Accredited Professional InterfaceFLOR

"Marj Barlow helps improve women's potential and quality of life. Her methodology brings dynamism and possibilities that outweigh the individual reading, going further providing the possibility to connect groups of women that can work together toward a more elaborate consciousness of their potential as human beings."

–Reinaldo Schwarz, Marketing Co-ordinator, Latin America, InterfaceFLOR

This book is an interesting mix of memoir and teaching. Her voice cuts thru all the clutter of the theoretical and gets to the heart of the matter."

–Vicki Duvuono, InterfaceFLOR

"Marj Barlow has generously shared with us a 'blueprint for living'. Ours is simply to understand, accept, adapt to our own, put into practice and pay it forward to all who come after us. This generous legacy is not only a precious 'liveable' gift to me but also will be to my children and grandchildren—'The circle of life'."

–Sheri Coveyou, RN

"The Possible Woman Steps Up, is very inspirational and motivating…"

–Luciano Bonini, Marketing Director, InterfaceFLOR, Latin America

"I smiled the entire time I read this book, even when I was covered with goosebumps or tears rolled down my cheeks. The smile was a result of more than merely being entertained (and I was), it was pure joy, because Marj was once again (just as with her first book, The Possible Woman) gently tapping into that space deep within my being that is so ready to open the door and step up."

–Cassie Schindler, The Alternate Path

"In the years that have known Dr. Marj Barlow, she has made leadership appear as natural as breathing and her new book, The Possible Woman Steps Up is no exception."

–DaAnna Stringer, da stringer designs, LLC

"Dr. Marjorie Barlow through her life and teaching has brought strength, purpose and, most of all, harmony to my life. I am grateful she has now written this book so that all women can thrive in today's world."

–Mary Davis, NCTM (Nationally Certified Teacher of Music)

The Possible Woman Steps Up

Also by Marjorie R. Barlow, Ph.D.

Couples Night Out: Four Dates A Year To Save Your Marriage
The Possible Woman

The Possible Woman Steps Up

Women's Leadership in the 21st Century

Marjorie R. Barlow, Ph.D.

BALBOA.
PRESS
A DIVISION OF HAY HOUSE

ISBN: 978-1-4525-4365-9 (sc)
ISBN: 978-1-4525-4366-6 (e)
ISBN: 978-1-4525-4367-3 (hc)
Library of Congress Control Number: 2011961864

Balboa Press books may be ordered through booksellers or by contacting:

Balboa Press
A Division of Hay House
1663 Liberty Drive
Bloomington, IN 47403
www.balboapress.com
1-(877) 407-4847

Because of the dynamic nature of the Internet, any web addresses or
links contained in this book may have changed since publication and
may no longer be valid. The views expressed in this work are solely those
of the author and do not necessarily reflect the views of the publisher,
and the publisher hereby disclaims any responsibility for them.

The author of this book does not dispense medical advice or prescribe the use
of any technique as a form of treatment for physical, emotional, or medical
problems without the advice of a physician, either directly or indirectly. The
intent of the author is only to offer information of a general nature to help you
in your quest for emotional and spiritual well-being. In the event you use any
of the information in this book for yourself, which is your constitutional right,
the author and the publisher assume no responsibility for your actions.

Any people depicted in stock imagery provided by Thinkstock are models,
and such images are being used for illustrative purposes only.
Certain stock imagery © Thinkstock.

Printed in the United States of America
Balboa Press rev. date: 12/12/2011

Contents

Introduction

The Possible Woman Steps Up is the sequel to my first book, *The Possible Woman.* I invite you, a woman of possibilities, to think about yourself as a leader. If you are male, I invite you to think of women who deserve your encouragement, support, and mentoring in leadership roles.

Women are ready. Women can do it. Women can change the world. This book is about you as an individual woman, connected to all women, and thereby connected to all life. You live in a sphere of individual influence, and with your leadership, this can be a world of peace, love, harmony, and human fulfillment.

Especially in the last half of the twentieth century, women have been preparing, directly and indirectly, to move into more visible roles as world leaders. My own career developed after twenty years of leadership as a mother. After vigorous study of psychology, theology, philosophy, and human development, I broadened my leadership role to include the larger community. I became a therapist, and I was "therapized." In the process, I both took and taught courses, workshops, and seminars aimed at self-help and personal growth. In all of these life-changing growth events, the majority (even 90 percent of the participants) were women—females—the fair sex, preparing (perhaps unconsciously) for leadership in the coming age. This book is about all of those women stepping up to their leadership potential, aware of their creative roles in our future life on this planet Earth. As we enter the next twenty-five hundred years of evolution, I believe that women will be leading the way—in feminine style—toward an ecologically, economically, and socially sustainable future.

I believe our lives are lived as dramas and that we are the creator of our story. My work as a therapist became my way of helping others get their own stories into forms they liked. Each of the chapters holds stories for your development. My website, marjbarlow.com, will have further exercises in workbook form.

There will be eight chapters in this book because of an eight-part joyful daily practice I do with my beloved husband. Picture two eighty-year-olds turning to the eight directions in a slow, mindful meditation that is like a body poem. As we turn to the southeast, I think of existence itself. Turning to the northwest, I feel caring and compassion. Shifting to the southwest, I think about creativity. To the northeast, I am one with all in our evolution. To the west, I ponder what it means for me to play. Turning toward the east, I think of learning and to the north, I name what I love. Our final turn is to the south, where I think of my work, which is my contribution to my world.

Stars are a reliable anchor in the world we inhabit. They are always there. My father-in-law said they are our friends. They are our neighbors. Because they are always present and we can count on them, I extended my thinking to include one star for each direction. I am but a grain of sand, a speck of dust in the vast universe, yet I comprehend that I am connected to all life. Our morning ritual is my reminder of that connectedness.

Chapter 1 begins with *existence* itself and acknowledges the rights of all women to sovereignty over their lives. The invitation to every woman is to *show up*, to risk her life to be an integral part of the course of human history. Chapter 2 is about *caring* and is concerned with the next phase of our brain development, the path of altruism and empathy. I urge you to *listen up*, with accurate ears and intuitive awareness. In chapter 3, we will look at the *creativity* of women and the potential for all women to add voices that speak for the good life of peace, prosperity, and harmony. This chapter calls for women to *open up* to their creative potential. Chapter 4 is a glimpse at the Aquarian Age of our *evolution* as human beings in general, and women in particular. The message in this chapter is to *grow up*. Chapter 5 is about *play* and speaks about the wisdom of not taking ourselves too seriously and the need to *lighten up*. Chapter 6 concerns *learning* and is about the joy of lifelong learning. The challenge is to *wise up*. In the last two chapters, we will remember Sigmund Freud's concept of the vital function of human life, which is to love and to work. *Love* means relationship with self and others, so we *link up*. *Work* is what we contribute as we *offer up*.

Each chapter can be a lesson or group study in leadership development for one woman or a circle of women. The chapters themselves make a great topic for a meeting of supportive friends. There will be instructions for preparation through mental focus and mind stretching on the subject, which can be followed by enjoyable dialogue using the workbook on my website, marjbarlow.com.

If you imagine that you are a tree, the "leafing out" amounts to mind stretching. As if you are reaching for more light, you can go beyond your edges. See the workbook at my website, marjbarlow. com, for help with your "root extension," as if you are planting yourself in your leadership role. Thirsty roots are akin to women's quest for leadership possibilities. My wish is that you and your circle of women friends can come together in wisdom groups for the best growth and development of each one who attends.

This is not a book about men being at fault. We have all come to this place, in this time, for very good reasons, and we will all go forward into the future with the power of our intentionality. Spending time or effort on blame and faultfinding is fruitless and not the goal. The goal is to offer inspiration, encouragement, instruction, and help for women. Every woman has unique qualities, her own original vision, and incredible determination. My wish is that each woman will claim her significance in this time and place.

Acknowledgments

I am in the last quarter of my life as I write this. In my final years of existence on earth, I share with Paul, my life partner, all the rich stories of our past and our present, and we create the best future possible until we take our final passage into the realm of the eternal souls that we both are. These are my dreams. My life is the legacy I leave to my family. These are all my heirs of fortune—my pay-it-forward legacy who will carry forth the truth as they see it and will deliver to their world the contribution that they each can bring. Only they as individuals can create that. I am also grateful for the short life of my first husband, James, who was the loving father of our first four children. His brief time on this planet was lived to the fullest, and his contribution will be part of my legacy forever. James Robinson, Ph.D. was a pioneer in the field of quantum physics, and Paul Barlow, Ed.D. is a pioneer in the movement toward positive psychology. I have had great help from both of these beloved husbands who shared their world and our life. My five children, Anna Brown, Mike Robinson, Kaye Barlow, Edward Robinson, Ph.D., and Cynthia Barlow, were part of the laboratory where I applied what I learned. I am eternally grateful for their love and support. I deeply appreciate their tolerance of my mothering, mistakes and all, and cherish the evolutionary contribution each of them makes to the future.

My colleagues at InterfaceFLOR are all cherished, supportive friends. I hold the warmest thanksgiving for their kindness and encouragement these past fifteen years. I have great faith in their leadership and know that this company is in good hands for a sustainable future.

I also leave this legacy to all those individual women who have trusted me by telling me their life stories. Each woman who reads my book can get a taste of what I believe, and from that she can develop what she believes. Then, by thinking it and dreaming it, she will create the next possibility, and our world on this planet will be changed toward positive and for the good.

CHAPTER 1:

Show Up

The Joy of Existence

Preparation for this chapter: Take a few minutes
for this "mind-stretching, leafing-out" process. Ponder,
meditate, or just be still while you notice your thoughts.
Think about how you are the Possible Woman and you
live on planet Earth, which is a part of the universe.
Literally turn your body to face the southeast.
Remember the myth of Persephone and your role as a
girl-child-daughter who has experienced your own trip
into the underworld. Color that world red. Imagine that
you can reach far, far into space, touching a distant
star. Let your vivid imagination take you to the star
named Rigel, the Traveler. This star forms the western
foot of the Hunter Orion, and its Arabic name means,
"Leg of the giant." Think of the star as a symbol of
you as a traveler embarking on your entire life journey.
Ask yourself to define your own giant legs. Allow your
inner little girl to feel those sturdy legs. Meditate on
the two words, "I am."

Marjorie R. Barlow, Ph.D.

Here I Am

I was born on the plains of Texas in my grandfather's farmhouse. There were four adults in my life, and I was the only child. They watched me a lot, so there was a big calamity on the day that they lost me. They were looking for me all over the house, in the closets, at the barn, in the toilet, behind the lilac bushes, and in the orchard. They were calling me by both my names, which is the real indicator of how serious this was. "Margie Ruth!" was being called loudly by Grandfather, whom I called Poppie Mac, Daddy, Mother, and Aunt Jimmie. Jimmie was afraid I had been killed and eaten by the hogs, and Poppie was getting ready to drag the waters in the tank, panic-stricken that I had drowned. My mother was walking around the far side of the house, and she heard a little voice saying, "Here me am." It seems I had crawled under the house and was having quiet alone time, away from all eight eyes watching my every move.

Our life stories unfold in fractal wave patterns, and this is one of those patterns in my showing up. I am still self-conscious today when I think people are watching my life with a judgmental mindset. I pick up intuitively when they are critical, and I want to hide out until the voice is warm, inviting, friendly, and accepting. My mother's voice calling my name was not harsh, but she spoke to me from her perspective of wanting me, cherishing me, and hoping to find me. So, I spoke up timidly, "Here me am." Then all was well. I was found, and they were relieved. Today, I still have that tentative voice speaking out, saying, "Here me am." My growth edge is to be willing to say clearly, even enthusiastically, "Here I am." With more than eight eyes watching, I desire to show up.

You have come into this life with a purpose. Stop for a moment to ponder what your showing up, or your mission in life, might be. To show up is to risk being your authentic self, your fullest possibility as a woman in this life. Are you ready to be CEO, CIO, CFO, doctor, professor, senator, judge, or any title that you like?

SHC was the job title chosen by Dianna (not her real name), a free-spirited woman who did all the necessary things in her small company. She made the coffee, kept the schedule, filed the papers, delivered the communications, and fixed the computers. She was the first one they thought of for any task. So, when her boss asked what title she preferred, Dianna answered whimsically, "SHC: Supreme High Commander." Then there was Georgia, another woman who did a different version of the necessary things. She built relationships, was present when there was a crisis, listened to everyone, and was interested in everyone. She kept the machinery of human interaction flowing in her world. When asked what title she wanted, she said, "President." Each woman was a leader who had her own style of engagement, Dianna as Dianna and Georgia as Georgia. They were engaged in living up to their maximum possibilities. Each of them took the risk of showing up.

Wisdom from the Past

We stand on the shoulders of the women who have blazed our trail. We inherit the knowledge and skills of our grandmothers. Thousands of women have been named in our history from the time of the early goddess cultures through our recent story of militant feminism. The evolution of women in the twenty-first century has been constructed from the lives of these forebears.

Martyred women, like Joan of Arc, sacrificed themselves for their cultural leadership causes. Hero women, like Elizabeth Cady Stanton, met the needs of their generation for female rights. Courageous women, like Eleanor Roosevelt, found a leadership voice from the template of their time. Intelligent women, like Benizir Bhuto, exercised their rightful places as leaders of their countries and died in that cause. Their stories are in our DNA. We share the makeup of their bodies, the pain of their suffering, and the outrage of their treatment. We are heirs to their intellect, determination, survival, and "thrival." Their wisdom, born of their experience, is passed on to us.

One of my workshops from the past was called, "From Rage to Courage, a Woman's Journey into Wholeness." My observation, based on the stories of my clients, was that when a woman got mad, her rage could quickly escalate into monumental proportions. One woman suddenly changed into a representation of the collective rage from all martyred, enslaved, abused, and captive women from ages past. It seemed as if those memories were somehow stored in the common DNA. At the same time, the men in her life, including her medical doctor, often found justification for her rage in hormones. Transforming rage into courage means doing something about the outrage. Candy Lightner and Cindy Lamb were two examples of women who turned rage into courage by founding Mothers against Drunk Driving. In warrior fashion, they turned their rage into a positive force for change. Mike Morrison, who served as the dean of Toyota University, says that real leaders bring about meaningful change. Women seem to have a knack for knowing what change will have real meaning.

Maybe now we won't be put to death for our heroism. Or will we? I had the privilege of spending a few hours in deep conversation with Benizir Bhutto when she spoke at the Possible Woman conference in Atlanta. She told me of the problems with her country, Pakistan, and of her sorrow about the plight of women. She and I shared our belief in the great life force. She was smart, well-educated, beautiful, and visionary. Her tragic death brought great sadness. I wonder if we can make the world safe for women to be visionary leaders. What meaningful change might have been brought about by women of the past if they had been allowed and empowered to lead?

We are here to heal the past, to envision the future, and to create a peaceful, joyful existence. Such an existence will not only bring women to parity but also release men to be fully human and fully alive. Each individual woman is significant and unique. It is that uniqueness and significance coupled with the oneness and sameness of all life that we are to engage. One woman engaged in the process of evolutionary change makes a difference.

Individuation

There is no other like you. Existence needs you. You are the Possible Woman, with your own individual differences and strengths. Your uniqueness is about the way you create your life, your style. It is apparent in the way you like to live, work, and interact. Every interaction shows your style. Who you really are is revealed in every conversation. We who have been doing Possible Woman seminars, events, and cruises for twenty years have asked two questions: "Who are you today?" and "Who can you become tomorrow?"

So, what is a leader? Specifically, what is a leader who happens to be female? More specifically, what are the possibilities for women becoming leaders in the United States of America and in our whole world? What kind of leader will the Possible Woman be? The answer to the question will be found in the ultimate development of individual women, who will imprint their styles of leadership on those they lead.

Servant Leaders

A servant leader of either gender rallies those who follow to: 1) higher and better performance, 2) more virtue in character, and 3) satisfaction of human needs. A leader is in position at the front, the vanguard, with a comprehensive view of what is demanded for her enterprise to be successful. She inspires loyalty and has a calming effect in the face of fears. Her enterprise may be her family or it may be a factory, school, church, or country. Whatever the enterprise, she can exert her influence. We are naturals in servant leadership, for women have done the necessary things to keep the human race progressing. Centuries of serving the good of the race resulted in a twenty-first-century model woman ready to take her place in leadership.

Visionary Leaders

Servant leaders can be of two types: visionary and managerial. There are visionary leaders who see the future with sharp clarity. They think in terms of possibilities, and they are dedicated to the creative *seer* role that shows the way and that guides the family, group, corporation, nation, or world. Such a leader is endowed with the qualities of the goddesses, Athena and Artemis. Such goddesses and gods from Greek, Egyptian, and Roman history were precursors for the science of psychology. We can learn about our personalities by studying them. Athena was the muse for Odysseus, and she invented things like the plow and other crafts. Athena is a prototype of the visionary woman who can see where we need to go. She can lend her voice to those who find the way, and she will lead by her brilliant ideas, plans, and strategies. Artemis is more revolutionary and really sees the need for women to have a new voice. Artemis was the goddess of the hunt and the moon and had her own territory. Each goddess is part of every woman. Each is ready to envision the future that wants to emerge.

Managerial Leaders

Another type of servant leader is the managerial kind. This woman is equipped to bring forth the goodness and strengths of others. She sees talent, she is optimistic, she has faith in people, and she knows how to bring out the best in those she manages. This type of leader is a master of task completion. This is sometimes a mother type, fashioned after the goddess Demeter. She is nurturing, selfless, giving, and caring. Her goal is to be compassionate, to help those who work for her to find their right seat on the airplane, to get into what they like to do best, and to encourage them to continue learning and growing. She is a great mentor. She holds the family or the organization together. She is a developer of people, whether they are male or female.

Either one of these types of women, visionary or the managerial leaders, will perform in leadership capacities provided they make the choice of being wholeheartedly engaged, which means responding to the needs around them. Buckminster Fuller said, "When you don't know what you want to do, look around and see what needs to be done. Choose from that list and get busy doing it!" A fully engaged woman can make things happen. She gets things done. She simply chooses to show up. She puts herself out there. Showing up in fullest mind, body, and spirit is the challenge. She can begin by not taking a backseat. She can risk finding her own voice in world affairs. She is you, and you can choose to never succumb to the "poor me" victimization voiced by men and women alike when things don't go their way.

To show up is to come into the workplace as a leader with enthusiasm, fully engaged and ready to be there in the now moment. The now moment is really all we ever have. To live in the past is to invite depression. What might have been "if only" this or that and the anger over past crimes against one's personhood are at the head of the list of ways to justify not showing up. Or the alternative might be living in the future, which guarantees worry and anxiety. Now is equivalent to eternity. Living in the now is the place where engagement happens, where we can step up to our leadership potential, and where we enter the flow of life.

Who Am I? The Clock of Awareness

What makes you tick? What ticks you off? Imagine for a moment that you are a clock. In our simple metaphor, twelve o'clock is the place where you store beliefs, the concepts that you hold certain.

Like the plot in a movie, beliefs are the moral of the story and represent your fundamental understanding of the nature of the universe and of yourself in relation to that universe. Those beliefs lead to three o'clock, where thoughts transpire. Thoughts include images and words that create the movie in your head, complete with narrator, commentary, and vivid pictures. Some thoughts may become so pervasive that they cycle like a bad rerun! Then proceed to six o'clock. Six o'clock is the place where emotions and feelings are stored. They are your life's sound track, flowing like music with life's ups and downs. Feelings have a distinct energy and movement associated with them. When people get emotional, they say, "That really moved me." At nine o'clock, imagine your behaviors showing up. Behavior is little more than the words we speak, the tone of voice with which we speak those words, our facial expression, our body postures, our gestures, our costuming (what we wear), and our movements.

The clock of awareness is like a cause-effect machine, with beliefs giving rise to thinking. Thoughts stimulate emotion, and emotion is like energy in motion, or our feeling flow. Feelings can provoke behavior. If you want to know how you got the feelings you are experiencing, look at the thoughts you have been having. And if you really want to know what sets it all in motion, examine your belief system. One quick way of knowing what your beliefs are is to observe your behavior, for behavior, verbal or nonverbal, gives away our beliefs. What we sincerely and deeply believe, we will create. Today's woman can change beliefs. From subservience to real service, from controller to developer, and from compliant follower to courageous leader—these are growth challenges for the Possible Woman.

Old beliefs about women's roles and distinctions about male and female are in the process of big change. My grandfather believed that women were never to wear trousers. His thoughts were governed by that belief; his feelings were upset whenever he saw a woman wearing slacks or God forbid, shorts. His behavior was to loudly and vehemently condemn such women. His clock of awareness was stuck in a past generation. Today, we have new beliefs, thoughts, feelings, and behavior about what women wear, but we still have beliefs that indicate men are never to wear skirts—kilts maybe, but not dresses.

Our patterns of thoughts, feelings, and behaviors are indicative of good things too. Our talents are recurring patterns of thoughts, feelings, and behavior. These talents are the indicator of what is good about both genders. Cultivating those talents into strong beliefs that are positive is a hallmark of women's leadership.

Our behavior tells the truth for us. Our nonverbal movements and gestures will often show what we believe in our deepest being. The body does not lie. If we are self-observant, we can know more about what we think and what we really believe about ourselves. Notice what you say, your movements, your gestures, your tone of voice, and your body posture, for they reveal the truth about your subconscious mind and what is true for you.

I remember the woman who wanted to save her marriage, yet she kept taking her wedding band off and putting it back on during the session. By calling her attention to that gesture, I gave her a chance to see what she really believed about her marriage. She was surprised to know that her nonverbal behavior was speaking to her unexpressed feelings. Her revelations led her to a new answer to the questions, "Who am I?" and "Who can I become?" It is through our desires that we form our intentions. Our intentions set in motion our design for life. And our life is our story lived daily, chapter by chapter.

The Clock of Awareness

Beliefs

Beliefs are what we hold to be true. Beliefs are connected to leadership. Since we transform from the inside out, our capacity for leadership will correlate with our capacity to transform ourselves. Beliefs hold what is certain to us. Beliefs can and do change. Our certainties change. What I believe today about life, others, myself, and things of a supernatural nature is open to my curiosity and my questioning. Some say our great-great-great-great grandparents believed that the earth was flat, and they thought there was an edge at the horizon where they would fall off the earth. They were afraid, and their behavior was in accord with their belief. That old, outmoded belief changed in the light of new knowledge.

I now believe that we change from the inside out. I share my personal journey as a way of giving permission for each woman to do likewise. Your life journey is your own, and your beliefs are your personal privilege, as well as your personal responsibility. All along the way, I have changed and grown as I examined myself. That means that my beliefs have also changed and grown. We are flexible and elastic in our mind-brain-heart system. Growth, change, and questioning of beliefs are ways we discover who we really are, the essence of our being. I believe that we lead when we work our transformational magic, for we will show up as authentic. We will provoke meaningful change. We will be changing, constantly transforming into our best possible selves. I am convinced that we see what we look for, not what we look at. We hear what we listen for, and we experience the consequences of our own beliefs, thoughts, and feelings.

Thoughts

Thoughts show up as internal words, sensations, ideas, pictures, and an ongoing stream of consciousness internally. I have learned to transform my internal chatter into a new version without fear, judgment, or blame. Old thought habits have been hard to break and have been worth the effort. When I am in my new patterns, I enjoy thoughts of love and forgiveness, compassion and caring, and creating and manifesting the good and the lovely. Truth, beauty, and goodness are thought forms. These are the major three from Plato: truth equals what science gives us, goodness is linked to religion and morality, and beauty is art. Learning is one of my strengths, and books are my addiction. Through reading and experiential learning, my thought process has transformed. Expansion of thoughts beyond the echo of my childhood experience is my individual evolution in action. Standing on the shoulders of those who gave me life, building beyond their dreams, healing the wounds they suffered and passed on to me, and forgiving and accepting with gratitude the journey up to now brings new thought filled with curiosity, wonder, awe, and amazement. From the refreshing field of new thought comes my creative expression of my true self.

I am a devotee of Byron Katie, who has given us her life-transforming method called, "The Work." She asks, "Do you believe your thoughts?" "What do you experience when you believe your thoughts?" and "What would you be without that thought?" Her method of inquiry is worth learning and applying to your everyday existence, one thought at a time.

Feelings

Feelings are body sensations. Emotional flow is energy in motion. Feelings are an authentic navigational instrument—a personal GPS. Negative emotions are signals that provide guidance. Like the guidance system on a car, they tell us when we need to make a u-turn. They signal that we are off the path of our positive energy flow. Feelings are the outcome of beliefs and thoughts. Self-pitying thoughts lead to depressive victimization. The victim voice tells victim stories, which guarantees continued bad feelings.

In my growth, I have discovered that I really can get beyond or below the victim story. I have learned to acknowledge and feel the energy. I can usually stop the "pain-body" stories of persecution and victimization. The feelings of joy are underneath all that suffering. Pain is a part of presencing, but suffering needs a story to keep it going. Pain is a given fact of existence, a signal in our earthly bodies, but suffering is an option, a choice, even a thought-form. My new thought patterns provide a path of positive awareness and action leading to transformation. I believe that new thought patterns, in each individual, can transform the path of all humanity. PAATH is a good acronym for creative output: Positive Awareness and Action Transforming Humanity.

Behavior

Behavior is what we do. What we say and what we do in gestures, movements, postures, and actions make up our behavior. Each of us can become more aware of our own facial expressions, our tone of voice, our speech patterns, and the "costuming" of our bodies. We can accept and work with the fact that we are in the process of creating a live human being, evolving through awareness and change.

I watch my behavior from a benign witness standing outside myself and looking on. The story is my most fascinating endeavor. Watching my own story unfold; taking responsibility for creating the drama; and then having fun on the stage of life makes for rich inner entertainment. Assuming full ownership of how I show up in daily life, especially with the ones I love dearly, is the greatest challenge and opportunity. If I take it very lightly, creating more of a comedy than a tragedy, I find it to be even more entertaining. At my most elevated evolutionary moments, I discover the wellspring of joy, which is my birthright.

Your Story

If you are ready to show up, then get ready for a time of real self-study. Authoring your own story means taking ownership of the plot as well as the action. Your stage belongs to you, even though there will be other actors on your stage. You can choose your responses, thereby proving that you have the power to be the leader in your own life. Presencing is a new verb that means to be alive in your own mind, body, and spirit. It means to claim the moment, feeling what you feel, being aware of your thoughts, observing your behavior without blame or judgment, and allowing yourself to take the high road in your self-creation. Presencing means that the hands on your clock of awareness always point to *now*.

You can join what I call the triple A and become the *author, actor,* and *audience* of your own life story. I invite you to show up, live in the present moment, stop all blame and self-pity, and assume your rightful place as a positive force in your world. You can do that if you elevate your awareness of beliefs, thoughts, feelings, and behavior. Awareness is the doorway to growth. Like a searchlight, your awareness will guide your thoughts. The part of you that is aware is that deep, sacred presence from the soul level of your being. The essence of who you are is held in the depths of your awareness, which is beyond your beliefs, thoughts, feelings, and behavior self.

Evolutionary growth for a woman ready to show up may involve a look at the past. The distant past includes such archetypes as the great Sophia, the divine feminine. Sophia was alluded to as the feminine face of God. It is no secret that we have been in an age of patriarchal dominance. The two or three thousand years of the Piscean Age are recorded evidence of our time in that stage of human history. The divine feminine has been "off-stage" for more than two thousand years and therefore not a part of mainstream religions on the planet. The early centuries of the Age of Aquarius are revealing new trends in human behavior. We now have women clergy, and most professions are balanced in the number of male and female leaders. The trend is away from patriarchal dominance. One woman who is a university president told me about the shock and awe of the faculty at another university when more women than men showed up for the veterinary medicine curriculum. She said the news created quite a buzz of excitement. We talked about the emergence of small pets as family members. The report was that women could not only care for the small animals but were also equally able to care for horses and cows.

Real Worth

To show up in full form, to be aware of one's intrinsic worth, to value one's efforts, and to place a monetary expectation on the marketplace for those efforts is the task for each individual woman. In my growing consciousness, I discovered that I had erroneously equated a person's worth with the amount of pay he or she received. Traditionally, women have been showing up to do the necessary things, such as childbirth, lactation, home-making, child-rearing, and tending the sick. Who decided that those activities were worth no money?

When do women decide that they are seven-figure beings?

What percentage of women on your company's board of directors are women? What percentage hold executive roles, and are those roles more in the arena of traditionally female jobs, such as human resources? Are women actually included in decision making at the top level? Showing up to claim our rightful inheritance, our rightful share of world wealth, and our rightful place in world power is imperative in this century.

What does one woman want? The age-old mystery question is answered in some fairy tales by the words, "sovereignty over her own life"—that's what a woman wants. So perhaps in some quarters of the world, we have now achieved sovereignty over our lives, but are we paid accordingly? And are we waiting for the men in power to make it happen, like the prince in the old fairy-tale about Cinderella? What can one woman do to bring us into gender-neutral parity? These are tough questions that the women of this first quarter of the twenty-first century are asking. Who will have the answers?

Leadership of Self

Sometimes when I am approaching sleep, just before entering that state of dropping off, I have this incredible sense of being totally safe. I am aware of being alive, of existing, of knowing that I am part of a bigger whole that I do not comprehend. Somehow, this feels like a starting point. Feeling safe and knowing that I belong to the human race serves to free me to become all I can become. I have the right and the responsibility to fulfill my mission. Coming to this profound sense of being, aware of my existence, and saying to myself, "I am" is a fascinating, remarkable quest. For all women (and men too), these rights and these responsibilities are ours. You can be a leader in your own development. You can be a leader who is clever and smart in your own world. You can be a powerful leader for a future that wants to emerge. This is what I mean when I say, "Show up!" You are not accidental. Without you, something is missing. There is no other like you. You are alive, and you are necessary to life. The next fifty years are still in the making. This future that wants to emerge needs your participation. Power of choice can be your rightful option. Asserting yourself is possible. You can follow your own inner voice, and happiness can be your choice. We can claim power as women and still have a positive, happy existence. You have the right to be as powerful as you intend. You also have the right to live in a state of joy. Indeed, your birthright is joy. Joy is found in existence itself. This leader inside you can joyfully show up on the world stage.

CHAPTER 2:

Listen Up

The Joy of Compassion and Caring

> Preparation: Look to the northwest, and imagine the
> star Antares, sometimes called the warrior. Think about
> joining with others in becoming a militant warrior for
> nonviolence and compassionate, unconditional love.
> Meditate on the phrase "militant compassion." Think
> about the words "I care" and what it means to be a
> leader who will listen up! As you envision a trip through
> space all the way to Antares, think the color orange and
> remember the story of Demeter, the great mother.

Transformation through Listening

My closest and most faithful support person is my husband, Paul.
He was my major professor in my master's degree program where
I studied the field of counseling and psychology. Paul taught me
about the positive approach to human development, which has
helped me in my work with business and industry. Our partnership
became a life journey in which we both have been transformed
in positive ways. He is so devoted to my development that he

has often joined me when I needed a partner in learning about how best to work with couples, families, and group and team relationships.

In 1989, we changed how we listen, which transformed our relationship. Paul agreed to join me in training as an Imago relationship therapist. Harville Hendrix and Helen Hunt pioneered a theory that became the best method I ever found for working with committed couple relationships. The theory said that we tend to marry people who are similar to our parents, with whom we struggle over issues that were unfinished in childhood. Basically, we fall in love with the person who is just right for provoking our leftover unfinished business from childhood. The basic skill was accurate listening or mirroring.

Paul and I were training in Imago Relationship Therapy at a hotel in Austin, Texas, with our teacher, Dr. Pat Love. Pat assigned a practice lesson in which we were to mirror each other's words over lunch. We were supposed to take turns talking and listening for ninety minutes. We walked across the bridge where the Austin colony of bats provides daily entertainment when they fly into the sky at sunset, arriving at Wyatt's cafeteria, which was packed with the Sunday lunch crowd. Lots of noise and many families were there, so our exercise in mirroring was to be a real stretch for us. We agreed to take fifteen-minute turns. He was first.

Paul said, "I think this is one of the silliest things we have ever done. We are both trained counselors, and we both know how to listen, so I don't really see how this will help us at all."

I was surprised at the feeling I had. Within a flash, I was feeling very angry. Here he was saying this was silly, and we had paid all this money to learn something new, etc. Time stood still. In a few split seconds of time, I raced through the resentful, angry feelings and actually did something that is still of benefit today. I set my feelings aside, put on my invisible protective Teflon armor, and became a flat mirror—a reflecting device. I discarded all my blame and judgment, and to my own amazement, I opened my mouth and said, "If I heard you correctly, you said that you think this is the silliest thing we have ever done. You said that we are both trained counselors and already know how to listen. You said that you don't think this will help us at all. Did I get it?"

He looked at me, paused, and said, "Yes, you got it."

Then I asked, "Is there more?"

He proceeded to tell me a whole lot more about how he really didn't think we needed this training. I held onto my accurate listener self and responded with sincere mirroring. He talked on for his fifteen minutes until he had no more to say about his resentment. Then he said, "It's your turn." I noticed his eyes were clear and seemed to invite me to really talk.

I said, "I felt some anger welling up when you first told me that you thought this was silly. But the more you talked, I found I could listen without immediately responding with my feelings, and I am glad now to know that I can do that."

Paul mirrored what I said, asked if he had heard me correctly, and invited me to say more. We continued to practice this new way of communicating, mirroring what each of us said until the crowd at Wyatt's seemed to disappear. We were in a cocoon of our own making, completely removed from the cacophony of the noisy cafeteria. At the end of the time, we were both clear, our eyes were seeing each other through wide-open lenses, our pupils had dilated (a sign of pleasure), and we were both in a state of high joy. We learned that reflecting could replace our old habit of reacting, arguing, and squabbling. Reflective listening filled up the hole in the middle of soul. We had discovered how to go deeper into our love relationship.

Necessary Skills for Leadership

Learning reflective listening is one of the best skills any leader can acquire. Women can learn this necessary skill, even if it is not always natural or easy. Women can be great listeners.

Most women know about caring and compassion because they have cared for the young. Mothering requires listening. The skills learned in mothering are transferable to leadership. Leadership skills include understanding the people we are leading. Reflective listening expands understanding. Leadership is further about seeing beyond the cutting edge, envisioning a better future. Leadership is about creating meaningful change. Effective leaders inspire their followers. Great leadership grasps the need for people to be well managed into their authenticity. Great leaders have faith that their followers want to make a contribution. Just as many mothers have been the inspiration and belief behind their children as they grow up, so it is with those who lead.

Managing people means developing people. Knowing their talents and focusing on expansion of that talent replaces the old path of fixing their weaknesses. Positive psychology aims at calling for what is good in people. Old-style psychology, based in pathology (disease), searched out what was wrong and attempted to correct it. We have many studies that refute the old "catch people when they are wrong" management styles. Learning to apply positive developmental methods is far harder than yelling at people to get them to act right. Jim Clifton, Chairman of the Gallup Organization, said, "If yelling worked, we would use that." Catching people when they are wrong, focusing on correcting mistakes, and shoring up weaknesses will not bring forth possibilities for optimum growth. People are meant to thrive, to flourish, and to grow. Optimism is superior to pessimism. These are beliefs that make sense to me, today. They are contrary to the prevalent thinking of my childhood.

Yet this is not a soft approach either. We expect much from people when we are accenting the positive. Listening with empathy is not the same as rescuing a victim, thereby creating dependency. Listening with empathy sets the bar very high. This type of leadership expects people to rise to becoming the very best version of themselves that they can imagine.

Three Needs

How can we offer this kind of development for those we lead? Human beings need three things to help them not only survive but actually to thrive. These needs were there at birth: 1) to be heard accurately; 2) to be seen through fresh, soft, loving eyes; and 3) to have a system of empathic support that will be there while we find our way to the next level of growth.

First, the baby would perish if someone did not hear and respond to its crying. The need to be heard does not end with childhood. We need to be heard in every stage of growth. Being listened to without judgment, blame, faultfinding, or "fixing" sets our course toward finding our own unique voice and expanding our essential true self. It is the basis for ownership of our fate and our existence. And if we own our existence, we come to the reality of being engaged. Engagement implies that we take 100 percent responsibility for our experiences. It is not a matter of getting a free lunch or an easy life, but rather it is that we grow into our best self when we are heard accurately, with respect and sincerity. I like to distinguish between my little, local, self and the best possible high Self. The little local ego-serving self may get caught in pleasing others, being perfect, being strong, or being careful. The capital-S Self is the essence of the true self. An engaged Self is enthusiastic, optimistic, and willing to "step up" to leadership roles.

Ask yourself, "Do I believe that human beings are born bad or good?" This basic belief is behind all our judgments. Can we trust that there really is a true high Self that indicates an essence of soul? Do you have a deep grasp of your own lovability? Can you look in the mirror at that reflection and say, daily, "I love you just the way you are"? My experience working with women is that they have many conditions surrounding their own self-love. One woman told me that when she looked in the mirror, she saw blemishes and frown lines. She actually talked about how she could not express self-love until she had a perfect face. (She was already scheduling cosmetic surgery.)

A woman executive told me recently that she would "always" tell her teenage son what he should or should not do because she was his mother. She was as stubborn about telling him as he was about rebelling against her. We discussed when he might be trusted enough to make his own decisions. She said she knew he was ready to leave the nest. She was still resistant to the idea that he was moving into his big breakaway into adulthood. Every conversation with him brought another angry scene. She said she wanted to let go, yet she feared he would fail unless she guided him. She also expressed her fear that he would be less than perfect.

I challenged her to stop criticizing and telling him what he should do for at least one week. She accepted the challenge and also expressed her new intention to learn to hear and understand him. She was willing to reframe the picture, seeing her son stretching into a new stage. She also became aware that he was facing his growth with more fear than his rebellious words were saying. As she herself grows, she is letting go of her need to control and transferring her trust to her son to guide his own life.

The same woman admitted that she had problems with her direct reports at work. She has been referred to as the quintessential micromanager. She admits it is the biggest challenge she has faced in all the years of her mothering and her managing. She saw the parallel to her managerial style and is becoming increasingly aware of how she manages people much like she mothered her son.

In the world of business, I see rebellious people who are disengaged because they, too, are being told what they should do rather than being invited to participate in the daily tasks of the job they are hired to do. The real advantage to being a leader who listens with compassion is that the followers, be they children or employees, will become engaged in the world they inhabit.

The mystery of accurate listening is the secret to many life solutions. Counselors who are successful use active listening in every counseling session. Active listening is nondirective and centered on the talker, not on the good advice that could be given by the listener. Good managers and great leaders listen to the world around them. The best managers I know are the most observant of the environment around them. Great leaders make a difference when they gather the information needed to understand the group, the individual, or the corporation. Listening without preconceptions or judgment promotes understanding.

Listening without fixing, without offering a solution, is the best kind. Why is that? The reason we need to be heard accurately without someone taking over and giving us a solution is that we need to develop our own problem-solving skills. We need to think for ourselves. Otherwise we become codependent non-thinkers and victims. When every person does this, we have the advantage of all the brains in the group. If listening is done to gain control, we limit the contribution from the other group members.

Accurate Listening

Did you grow up in a non-listening family, where everyone simply talked louder than the other family members? Or maybe yours was a family where the father's voice was the dominant sound. For many years, I have helped families learn the skills of good listening. These skills are essentially the skills displayed in those primitive women circles. They can be learned even if family patterns and habits are not in alignment.

A man named Jeffrey who talked and talked and talked was one of my clients. I asked him, "Do you think I am hearing what you say?" Jeffrey thought a few moments and said, "Not really. Nobody ever listens to me." We explored the roots of that habit and found that, in his large family, everyone talked loudly and interrupted so that there was a constant game of "Uproar." His office reflected his family-of-origin's game. When Jeffrey learned to listen without blame, judgment, faultfinding, or fixing, things began to flow more smoothly. He stopped his volatile rage and his yelling. His office changed. The people working there began to feel safe and as a result, they became more engaged on a daily basis. Their productivity went up as well. Predictably, profits began to rise. Jeffrey found it difficult to believe that he could make such a difference just by changing his style to twice as much listening as talking or yelling.

Some of the people I have worked with seem to believe that listening is not really helping. Husbands and men typically are "doers." The belief is that unless you take some action, give some advice, or solve the problem, you are not really helping. If you are one of those people, consider that accurate listening is really an action designed to do something beneficial. If you need more listening skills, take a course and learn how to do it. Through our daily relationships, we get our lessons for growth in life. At home, at work, or in our community, we are stretched to our limits through our relationships. They are the secret to our evolutionary growth, evolving us to higher levels as we learn how to love one another. Relationships are the cogs in the gears in an expanding life. Listening is the grease that makes those cogs turn smoothly.

You, as an emerging woman of leadership, can listen up. You may have been doing so naturally all your life. If it is not your nature to listen up, I hope you will learn the skills. If you are an emerging twenty-first-century male, you can also learn these skills. Safe and compassionate listening is the foundation for peace in our world, which begins at home with those we call family.

Imago Relationship Therapy offers a method of listening called "The Couples' Dialogue," which will be described in a later chapter. If you learn how to reflect the words you hear (mirroring), it will be a rare gift to give another human being, for it helps them to: 1) hear themselves, 2) clarify their meaning, 3) move on to the next experience, 4) get relief from "stuffed" feelings that have not been expressed, and 5) move into the present moment in their full life expression, thereby becoming more of who they really are.

Seeing through Fresh Eyes

To be responsible for our own thinking, feeling, and behavior is encouraged and fostered when another compassionate human being sees us through clear eyes. We start every success with a now moment. We cannot succeed if we are identified by the actions of our past. One of my daughters wisely said, "I don't want to be the kind of person who spends her life lamenting that her brother took away her yo-yo when she was seven years old." She was declaring the end of her own victimization with that statement. Soft eyes are the kind of eyes that give the benefit of the doubt. My grandfather saw me through fresh and loving eyes when I was six years old. I had lied my way out of a jam, and he simply said, "Little tongues do slip." This horrible crime I had committed was absolved, and I became new again through his compassionate seeing of me. His wisdom said I was incomplete—simply not done yet. He gave me permission to say, "Oops," and try again.

I challenge myself to see my family members through new eyes, as if they were strangers unknown to me. This exercise has helped me to learn more about how to understand and love. The old and outmoded habit is to think we know them. We might have known them as they were yesterday, but today is new. We can freshen our own eyes to see them as different than they were yesterday. Every moment is a new beginning. We didn't perish from the mistakes we made, so we can interpret our mistakes as a part of an experiment in learning in this laboratory we call life. We are not done yet!

I told a group recently that I have a very happy marriage because I have a new husband every day. One man said, "You go, girl!" I explained that every morning when I greet Paul, I see through fresh eyes, without prejudice about his past behavior. He also views me through renewed vision every day. We have adopted a belief that our past mistakes offered opportunities for learning but did not really define who we were. We continue to be works in progress. Economist and Nobel prize-winner Daniel Kahneman established that there are twenty thousand moments every day in which we can make choices about our world and the people in it. We can choose to see ourselves or others, without judgment, blame, or faultfinding. We always have a choice of the two paths: optimism or pessimism. I am convinced that optimism beats pessimism in terms of forwarding human evolutionary growth.

Holding the Field

Babies need to be held. Physical holding and human touch is necessary for babies to thrive. The same need is still present in us as adults. Holding can be nonphysical, as when we have a time of failure and someone's kind words are as comforting as arms around a baby. For anyone in a leadership position, not everything will go according to plan. Sometimes we have to stop and regroup. When we have a bad day, every individual needs someone or a group of someones to "hold the field" while they recover and find their way back to center. Holding the field might mean being present while anger is expressed, without consoling, shaming, or demanding that the anger be over too quickly. To make it safe for expression of any feeling is to hold the field. When we cry, we need someone who has a box of tissues ready to use, not placators or cajolers who want us to get past the feeling quickly. This is the real meaning of respect. The word itself means to look again. Respect given and respect received become possible through nondirective listening, clear seeing, and patient holding, metaphorically, of the moment in time.

Rule of Thumb for Listening

One of the first things to learn when we are working with other people is exactly who owns the problem. A simple rule of thumb is to first decide what is being expressed. If the need is for information, the listener may become a teacher or advisor helping to find a source for solution. If the problem seems to be all about feelings, then here is the rule. *Feeling problems belong to the one who is experiencing the feelings.* When feelings are being exploded or expressed, then the listener shifts into reflective mode. Our tendency is to alleviate our own discomfort by quickly offering a solution. Basically, we want them to move past the feelings. So we placate, reassure, offer advice, express sympathy, and cajole, sending the message to get over it and feel better now. Discomfort with negative feelings is understandable. It helps to really get clear who owns the feeling.

Negative feelings are an indicator that we are off-track and not operating from our native talent base. We can help each other express and clear negative feelings through deep listening. Feelings are very subjective, and they will change, given a chance to be "aired out" or expressed in a safe setting.

To be heard, seen, and respectfully supported is to be invited to grow in a world where someone cares, someone is compassionate, and someone empathizes. These givers of care, compassion, and empathy are the leaders who engage in bringing us to our fullest talents in operation. To listen may be the greatest act of leadership ever known. How many effective leaders do you know who are also good listeners? Those same leaders set high standards of excellence. Without using words, they communicate that they believe the people they manage are capable of delivering excellence. Most of the women leaders I have studied seem to set the standard of excellence by modeling it.

Twenty-First Century Women

We are at an expanded version of human history in the beginning of the twenty-first century. Cultural geography, the media, and communication have created a world that listens. We were traveling in the mountains of Mexico and marveled at how every mud hut seemed to have a television antenna. My friend talked

27

with his son who was traveling in Asia, halfway around the world, on his cellular phone. He remarked about the real magical times we are in. Information flows faster than ever. Today we hear and see through the genius of satellite communication that hooks us up as if the earth herself has a brain, and the neurons are now connected. No longer are we in the dark about what is happening to the cultures of our planet. One recent story told how the aboriginal women of Australia kept their tribal customs going even though they were not even counted as citizens of their country until fifty years ago. Citizenship was offered to these tribes in Australia at almost the same time we, in this country, were expanding our understanding of civil rights and apartheid in Africa was ending. Secrets of oppressive regimes are now subject to the scrutiny of the whole population. Our planetary tribe of humans is getting more aware of each other.

Leadership the Feminine Way

Women are informed. Women are poised and ready to assume leadership. Leadership, the feminine way, will be more horizontal and circular. Equality and inclusion are two ingredients in the way women lead. Women's circles are part of the new cultural geography, and they have been a part of women's history. Just as we sat together under the trees during our menstruation period on beds of moss in primitive ages when women entrained to the rhythms of nature, so it is today in dormitories where women, living together, seem to have moon periods at the same time. Those ancient entrainments expressed through circle customs, born of the nature of our bodies, have set the DNA for leadership, evolving into the circle way instead of the triangular, pyramidal, hierarchical leadership of the past centuries.

Compassion, circles, ritual communion, and inclusion are the results of eons of women's development. We can now empower young girls through education, and they will change the world with feminine-style leadership. Those young girls, growing up with full citizenship, belonging on the world stage, and bringing the wisdom of the ages learned by women who were behind the scenes doing the necessary things to keep life together, can be the new picture of the Aquarian age of information and ideas. There exists in women's circles a new kind of equality where each person leads in her own individual manner. When women feel themselves wrapped in a blanket of worthiness, they show up with inborn capacity for deep communion through listening. Compassionate listening comes from the very nature of women because our bodies are the source of gestation, birth, and nurturing our human species. We are mammalian and warm-blooded. We can transfer our accumulated wisdom to gestating and birthing a new age for our planet. It is our nature to listen, observe, and hold the field.

Women Leaders

Compassionate listening is a pattern that exists in women who are leaders. I have had the privilege of knowing some outstanding women leaders, and I discovered that they had some common characteristics among them. First, they learned about their world—through formal or self-directed education. They usually had a mentor who removed the barriers of old beliefs about traditional roles for women. One such woman had a grandmother who took over when her husband died and commanded a very large work force successfully. Another was unsuccessful in her marriages and reared her children as a single parent. The third woman started her own business after her children left home. Each of these women had unique skills, but they held in common one paramount skill: unusually keen listening. As they developed the people who directly reported to them, each woman told me that she gave credit to her own listening skills for her success.

The second characteristic these three women described was their love of people just as they are, without the need to improve. Each described herself as someone able to tolerate, even champion, diversity in any form. They spoke of the thrill of getting to know the personalities of the people they mentored. An accepting person sees us through eyes of nonprejudice. Prejudice means prejudgment. To be seen without past opinions or our mistakes being used as our identifiers is to be allowed to grow beyond those mistakes.

Foundational Ideas for Transformative Listening

Desire. To be a great listener, you first of all must want to hear what is said. This seems obvious, but tone of voice, facial expression, body posture, and gestures will send the truth to the talker.

Interest. You cannot fake being interested. If you do, the talker will sense your attitude and shut down. It is impossible to fake legitimate interest in another person. Insincerity seems to be instantly transmitted like a laser beam. The talker may still respond, but there is a subtle guard drawn up that acts as a shield around self-revelation.

Trust. If you are doing sincere deep listening, people open up and trust you with everything. There is such profound trust that building a deep relationship becomes possible from the very beginning.

Safety. Just as babies seem to have a sixth sense telling them they are safe with some people and not with others, so it is with grownups. This is the best cue to all women aspiring to leadership. Grownups are babies in disguise, and they will know at some visceral level whether or not you will treat them with respect and give them dignity. They will also know when you are judging them.

Deep Listening Means Caring

Seeing through eyes of acceptance means seeing through the filter of compassion and interest. Holding the field while someone finds the way to a brighter light is the ultimate charity. I hold beliefs that have evolved from my childhood learning. Much of that learning came through unnecessary pain, for a growing child whose brain is not yet developed does not need punishment. That growing child needs compassion and protection while she learns to trust, to explore, to invent, to create, to master skills, and to arrive at her teens with a clear picture of a positive identity.

I learned from my husband's practice of child-centered play therapy that children are asking three questions: "Do I belong?" "Can I cope?" and "Will I survive?" I suggest that is also being asked by anyone entering into conversation that holds meaning for the talker. When the listener implies the answer is yes, then trust is established. The listener silently says through nonverbal communication, "You belong," "You can cope," and "You are safe with me." That is the essence of transformative listening.

Your Worldview

You are living according to some belief you have adopted, which is either in the direction of "People are basically good" or "People are basically evil and must be controlled." The irony is that whichever you believe about other people is the belief that predicts how you view yourself.

We see the world through the filters of our belief system, and we apply that same system to ourselves, inside or outside. "Bummer!" you say? Yes, if you want to know what you believe, look at what you do. If you want to know who you are, look at the people around you, and ask yourself what your opinions are of them. We project our inside world into the outside world. We see what we want to see, not what we look at. We hear what we expect to hear, not the accurate reflection of their words. We experience what we expect, not what we say we want.

If what they are saying or doing does not look like love, it is best interpreted as a cry for help. This makes compassionate listening easier. Believing the world is friendly rather than hostile; being optimistic rather than pessimistic; and being mostly positive instead of negative all help with the skill of listening. Creative women leaders don't spend time and energy on telling victim stories. Aware and caring women leaders will show up for life, live compassionately, and courageously bring forth their truth without regard or attachment to any outcome.

Do compassionate love and caring really bring change? I believe they are the only way to bring lasting change. Violence does not do it. If so, our prison systems and wars would have produced some form of beginners' heaven on earth.

Women in leadership will face the great problems of humanity. War, peace, hunger, environmental sustainability, exploitation of resources, and a myriad of growing needs are the challenges of all world leaders. As I write these words, we still cannot find a path to peace. My optimistic view is that we are simply not done yet. As a human race, we are still in adolescence. My hope is built on my belief that we humans can grow up. Instead of living in fear, we can learn to love one another. I believe it to be true of individuals as well as of the whole of the human species that we are incomplete. We are evolving, and we can evolve to a more mature state.

Women can help. We are deeply connected with all life. We can have universal compassion and still be individuals who care about other individuals. The real capacity we hold is to do both. We can be one and we can be separate. We can be detached, and we can enjoy attachment. Universal compassion is our possibility. Individual affection is our privilege in our separateness as unique individuals.

We must listen to ourselves as the individuals we are with loving acceptance. We cannot love others until we love ourselves. Self-acceptance, self-love, and self-forgiveness are component parts to being caring leaders. This is not narcissism. This is being responsible for all that we as individuals do, all we think, all we feel, and all we believe.

To care as a leader, without falling into depression or sympathy, is to be mature and confident. To trust intuition and discernment is to be a leader who makes wise choices. To listen in the way that builds lasting relationships guarantees that there will be followers of our leadership. We are discovering the healing power of love and the advanced thought that we might actually create a world of nonviolence. We have tried the violent path to human solutions, and now we are ready to try another way. The way toward love in its truest sense means that we shift our beliefs to offering charity toward all. All is a very big word. It includes you. Giving caring and compassion to oneself is the paramount action to take first. Listening to the Self inside is necessary. Loving self makes you ready to love others. Deep listening to self and others, seeing through new eyes, and holding the field ensure that we will find our way to a future that wants to emerge.

CHAPTER 3:

Open Up

The Joy of Creativity

Preparation: Turn your body to face the southwest, and center yourself as a citizen of the entire universe. Imagine that you can reach out to the star Regulus, which means the heart of the lion. Think about the Lion in *The Wizard of Oz*, who wanted courage. Practice the statement, "I am a courageously creative woman." Say it, think it, feel it, sense it, and know it until you believe it. You are a courageous creator. Breathe in and breathe out as you affirm your new belief. The color is yellow, and the mythological goddess figure is Dianna (the Roman goddess or Artemis from Greek stories), the goddess of the hunt and the moon. This is your time to think about yourself as an independent woman, a midwife, a courageous leader. You as leader can be vulnerable as well as creative. You are traveling on your own yellow brick road to your own future.

My Story: Creating and Crafting My Life

My creativity was held in the boundaries of expectations born of my times. I was born in 1929, the year of the Wall Street crash that heralded the Great Depression. Women were not the financial leaders of that world. Women were not political leaders, medical healers, or religious experts. The majority of women were confined to the roles dictated by the female body. We were expected to stay home, marry and have children, tend the home, and volunteer in the community. Our professions were limited to teaching, nursing, or tertiary business positions, such as secretaries and clerks. My mother's generation got the right to vote when the Nineteenth Amendment was passed in 1920. The women who sacrificed to lead the nation into that are not remembered like the founding fathers, yet they were vital leaders who suffered for women's suffrage.

So as my story unfolded, I decided to be a secretary. By the time I reached thirty, I obtained a degree in business, married, birthed four children, helped my first husband get his PhD in theoretical physics, and built six houses, and I was living the life of a university professor's wife. I was president of the Faculty Wives Club. Then he suddenly died, and along with him, "our" PhD. I was alone in my world without his salary or credentials. My children might as well have been orphaned. Their daddy had died, and their mother was bereft. I still wanted to be a wife, and I wanted my children to have a father. I also needed to be able to support my family in case I could not remarry. I am telling this story now as a way of illustrating the miracle of manifesting the power of creating one's own life. My imagination, my journal writing, my thoughts, and my dreaming were all in the interest and desire for these three desires—another house, a master's degree, and a new husband. I created all that within three years. Whatever we think about tends to come about. The miracle of manifesting is in our mind. We can picture what we desire. We can intend the realization of that desire. It all starts in vivid imagination. Our creative power can manifest what we imagine.

Fast-forward several years. I am a wife, a mother, a counselor, and a very busy woman with a new husband, another precious child plus the first four equally precious children, and living in a new, larger home. I have emerged from the sorrow of losing a husband, survived widowhood, obtained another husband, and gotten another degree. We have created a community-counseling agency, and I am training to become a licensed marriage and family therapist. I am expanding my roles. Still a wife and mother and family-centered, I want to become an expert in family relationships. So here is the scene with the story I want you to know about creativity—about opening up to possibilities.

Picture a group therapy meeting. It is my turn to "work." I tell them that I have a real concern since Paul, my husband, is sick and undergoing some medical tests. I have a fear that he will get sick and die. The therapist asks, "What would you do if Paul died?" I replied that I couldn't even think about that. He insisted that I answer, and I began to grieve, saying, "I couldn't stand to lose another husband."

The therapist pressed on with insisting I look at what I would do if Paul died. After crying awhile, I could see that I would return to school and get my own PhD. I uncovered some very limiting beliefs in that therapy setting. Belief number one was that I must always be less than my husband, meaning I should be shorter, younger, and less educated. If he held a doctorate, then I could only have a master's-level degree. These were hidden deeply in my shadow, which is the dark, repressed material that we store in times when we are vulnerable and need to survive. Bringing irrational beliefs to the surface is one of the best forms of freedom for women. The strange thing that happened was that within two weeks of opening my mind up to these deep limiting beliefs, I was offered two opportunities to go forward toward my own PhD. The miracle was invited by my mind. I assisted by doing my own "stretching." I was changing a deep-rooted, old belief. There were many doubts and some fears along the way. I would write my name followed by the letters PhD over and over and over. I kept my positive energy going in the direction of what I wanted. It came about just as I imagined it. The moral for you is that you can stretch beyond your boundaries. You can create the dream of your life into the form that you desire. Your own mind will deliver whatever you generate from it. You can also dream of lack and limitation, and that will be yours just as surely as your positive dreams can be yours.

Beliefs are just thoughts we think a lot. Thoughts provoke feelings, which provoke action. The real key is, what are you imagining? Listen to your internal flow—the chatter of random thoughts and the picture of random images. You always have choices. Taking charge of our own awareness is the beginning.

Creativity or Reactivity?

Creativity and reactivity are spelled with the same letters. They are opposite sides of the coin of optimum human development. As long as we *react* to the stimuli that come our way through eyes, ears, nose, mouth, and skin, we will continue to be at the mercy of things outside of us. Reaction gives away power. Creativity claims power. We learned as children to survive in the world through reacting. It is a necessary and natural state since we humans are born dependent. For at least seven years after birth, we needed other human beings to nurture us. In the most natural reaction to our caretakers, we caught on to what was acceptable and what was not. Our parents, usually kind and caring, were mere mortals who imitated their own parents. Many of the nonverbal messages came to us in their reactions to our needs.

By the time we reached seven years of age, we had a fairly well established pattern of reacting. These patterns were generally in the form of internal motivators. Taibi Kahlor is a therapist and business consultant who devised the notion of five of these motivators. He called them drivers and categorized them as: be perfect, be pleasing, be strong, try hard, and hurry up. He offered the idea that we were, of necessity, programmed to react to outside voices and nonverbal communication. My study of transactional analysis gave me the understanding of these drivers as our counter-injunctions. The injunctions were absorbed in the nonverbal world of our childhood. We learned to counteract injunctions that were mainly expressed as don'ts. The drivers are our attempt to survive and outsmart the original messages, conveyed in such a way that we felt inadequate. Learning about one's life is the best thing we can do in opening ourselves to being creative. Nothing we have learned up to date is wasted. We survived, and here we are now, alive and ready to grow. Our creativity was dampened, if not cancelled, through all the survival mechanisms. Whatever it takes to uncover our self-limitations is worth doing. We are not victims, and we can open to our individual authentic, creative flow. Each of us is unique, different, and ultimately creative.

Instead of being perfect, I invite you to accept your mistakes as turning points in your growth. You are unfinished, and you are not done yet! Give up the need to please others, and notice what pleases you. You can accept and normalize the pleasure principle. You can let go of being strong and let yourself be weak at times. Let others do the heavy lifting, at least some of the time. Instead of trying hard, just do it, and instead of hurrying, you can stop, breathe, relax, and do things in your own time. Be aware of your instant reactions to outside energies. Stop and return to your own center of being. How can you center yourself? Breathe in and breathe out, relax, and love yourself just the way you are. Invite your creative juices to show up as you open up.

RIGHTS

In our natural state, we humans can generate thoughts and actions from the inside out. Our own internal drives, urges, beliefs, and responses are where personal power lies, not in getting change to happen in the world outside us. We can be in that internal drive—in the flow of energy that is unique and significant to each one of us. We have the right to change our locus of control from outside to inside.

To claim that right and get into that flow, we start with awareness. Awareness is like a searchlight. Whatever we shine the light on becomes the reality we experience. Awareness comes in through our senses. Be aware of what you are seeing, hearing, tasting, touching, and smelling right now. You have just centered yourself in readiness for the next creative impulse.

We are expressions of a creative life force, which means that we are also creators. Expand your definition of creativity. Creativity is the ability to generate innovative ideas and manifest them from thought into reality. The process involves original thinking and then producing our creativity through action. Thought provokes action. Imagination allows for creative thought. Vulnerability allows for creative action.

Action is behavior, and behavior includes what we say and our tone of voice, facial expressions, gestures, movements, and body posture. Behavior reveals beliefs. Change of belief brings lasting change. If you can believe that you are a creative person, you will discover many ways in which you have imagined something and brought it to pass. Einstein said that imagination is our greatest power. Imagination is our mechanism for original creative thought.

Imagery multiplied by vividness equals reality. What we imagine and what we think about comes about. Thinking makes it so. Motivational speakers have taught us that if we want to get something done, simply "Ink it! Think it!" and it will happen. Write down your dreams, accept your vulnerability, and stay focused on the desires that come from within you. If you examine your life successes, you may discover that your thoughts have brought about your reality. Your own imagination is the source of your greatest productivity.

If thinking creates reality, then why do we allow runaway thoughts to continue to keep us beaten down? Women especially seem to still honor old, outdated, and detrimental thoughts and beliefs. Changing beliefs is difficult yet worth doing. A change of belief brings change of thoughts, feelings, and behavior. Beliefs are just thoughts we think a lot, so change depends on thoughts that show up in words and pictures in our mind. Our creativity is anchored in what we believe, think, feel, and do. Creativity is a part of our human birthright.

How do we unleash this natural creative force that is part of our birthright? Glad you asked! Creativity shows up when these conditions are provided:

- Acceptance without judgment, faultfinding, blame, or criticism.
- Forgiveness when judgment, faultfinding, blame, and criticism have been the norm.
- Being in the now moment.
- Stopping assumptions.
- Not taking *anything* personally.
- Transforming the drivers (please, be perfect, be strong, try hard, or hurry up) into permissions to please yourself, see your mistakes as experiments, accept perceived weaknesses, take your time, and do what you desire.
- Attention, awareness, awakeness, and aliveness as an ongoing way of life.
- Transforming oneself through new ideas.
- Discovering the power of your own intentions.
- Recognizing that emotions are a guidance system.

Reactivity shows up when these opposite conditions are present:

- Constant appraisal (judgment that is either negative or positive).
- Faultfinding, blame, and criticism for what we do.
- Lack of forgiveness.
- Holding on to the past and letting the past define everything.
- Living in the past, which brings depression.
- Living in the future, which brings anxiety.
- Assuming you know what another is thinking or feeling.
- Taking everything personally.
- Believing, "It is all about me."
- Living in the trancelike illusion, being unaware, being asleep, and waiting for life to happen.
- Ignoring the vital signal sent by a negative emotion.

Fear is the basic negative emotion. The deepest fear is that we are not adequate, not enough. There is great vulnerability when we risk putting our ideas out there. Most of us have held back for fear that we will be judged harshly, ridiculed, or rejected. Reaction to the outer world prevents the flow of creativity from the inner world.

Responsibility—Energy in Motion

Each woman and each man has the responsibility for his or her clock of awareness. Ownership of our beliefs, thoughts, feelings, and behaviors is paramount for leadership development. It is the crucial factor for women stepping up to leadership. The energy in the clock of awareness is like a fuel tank. Positive emotions are the juice that fills the tank. Negative emotions affect the vehicle—the physical body. Like rust, wear, and breakdown of a bicycle or car, our negative emotions are hard on the body. What we feel, our emotional flow, is the indicator of being on track or off track in our creative development. We can be sure that we are on our path of highest development when emotions are positive. Negative emotion is only a signal. Heed the signal, and get back in the flow. Then creativity will abound.

It is our own responsibility to learn and do. Our personal flow of feelings belongs to us, not to someone else. Taking responsibility for this great change will create a positive direction for you in your journey to authenticity. The key is awareness of feelings. Ownership of feelings means accepting responsibility for any emotion we experience. Positive feelings are good (on track), and negative feelings are bad (off track). I admit that this is advanced development for humans and not easy to do. I made a living off of negative emotions in my work as a marriage and family therapist. The history and internalization of abuse, neglect, or exploitation is not something I take lightly or write off as easy to change. I have the greatest empathy for anyone, including myself, when we are stuck in the old story and cannot seem to quit telling the same poor, pitiful-me tale. We stop creating anything positive. And my best-worst client is myself!

I now believe negative emotion goes straight to the cells in the body in a distress reaction. Every malady known to us has a component of psychosomatic reality. We cannot separate psyche from soma (mind from body), and what we believe affects the cellular makeup of our bodies. Whenever we experience any negative emotion, our "fuel tank" is empty and we are out "pushing the car." Creativity has stopped because we are in protective mode. Body and mind work together to keep everything functioning. Creativity thrives in an integrated mind and body. Experiments with cells in Petri dishes shows that whenever something toxic or negative is introduced, the organism goes into protection mode. We do the same. Creative forward motion stops when we go into protection or defensiveness. We are responsible for changing, or we can express the darkness creatively. Even in expressing the dark side, we must become vulnerable and open.

Mental Rehearsal

When we focus our minds, turning the spotlight of awareness on some productive and positive possibility, creativity is invited to flow. When we allow our imaginations and our thoughts to expand into possibilities, we open the floodgates of creativity. The best way to do this is to watch your thoughts. Deliberately take charge of the thoughts and images in your mind, and mentally dwell on the thing you want to create. Mentally, rehearse the best possible outcome. See it, think it, imagine it, and make a delicious daydream of it. Let it be created inside your mind before you risk exposing it to the outer world. When we risk vulnerability and go ahead with revealing our ideas, we invite the expansion of human evolution to express through our one-person adventure. Sharing your creative dream with trusted friends is safe. Avoid anyone who wants to give helpful criticism or advice until the dream is anchored in your mind. Your creativity is like a fragile child who needs your care until it grows into its own pattern. Mental rehearsal of the desired dream is like in-utero cocooning, allowing your pregnancy to come full term and be ready to be seen. Your creative project is like the birth of a baby. It is protected and nurtured until it is full term, and then you can risk showing it to the world.

Relax and Wait

All creativity takes time. While you wait, you can continue to be aware of your own mental process. To encourage the flow of individual, unique creativity, dwell on these thoughts, mentally rehearsing them until you are able to internalize them as your own:

1. *Accept* your savant status. We are all geniuses in some form. You have natural talents that were formed before you were fifteen years old. Remember your uniqueness and your significance. You are here for a purpose that only you can fulfill.

43

2. *Live your life* congruently as a creator, believing that creation continues through you. Each of us has original vision, genius possibilities, and incredible determination.

3. *Risk entering* the unknown. Construct a place in your mind of high vibration and safety. Wait in silence and anticipation.

4. *Allow* the life force energy, your personal muse, your guides, angels, powers, ancestors, spirits, fairies, sprites, divas, photons, and all light beings to come into your state of presence. Presencing is a skill that can be learned, cultivated, and enhanced.[1] It means being in the now moment, fully present. I get to this place through awareness of my breath. Breathe in. Breathe out. Be here—*now*.

5. *Stay* in the process without interfering through judgment, control, or any form of evaluation. Anticipate inspiration, healing, and positive energetic flow. Flow is the unimpeded energy of the life force.

6. *Respect* whatever shows up. Creation is dynamic, fluid, and ongoing. Respect means "look again." So, look again at what you are creating and appreciate it.

7. *Empower*, enhance, and expand the process through open-ended questions and gentle curiosity, with anticipation of miracles. Keep anticipation in the most positive form. Creative tension moves toward whatever you anticipate. What you think about comes about.

8. *Patient waiting* for inspiration, resonance, and that electric and joyful feeling of discovery when a new idea shows up or a spurt of imagination gushes forth.

---

1   For more on presencing, read the book, *Presence*, by Peter M. Senge, and the Society for Organizational Learning, *www.solonline.org*. Other excellent books include *The Power of Now* and *A New Earth* by Eckhart Tolle.

Allow the delicious pleasure of following this muse from inside you. Give expression through whatever means come to you. Write a poem, paint a picture, color in a coloring book, make a garment, paint your walls, prepare a new recipe, or experiment with music. Anything that seems fun and playful can be a wellspring of creativity for you.

9. *Gratitude* expressed for the gifts of your own creative flow.

Application of this process, however it seems appropriate and actual to each individual, will produce an inspired possibility. All these inner constructs are part of each individual person's structure of consciousness. You can ponder these ideas by expanding your mind and stretching into your authentic self. Our limitations are all inside, not from the outside.

Intention

Creativity involves both intention and attention. It seems to flow from a wellspring within and is as individual as we are all different from one another. At the same time, we are all alike in many ways. I offer this example of giving attention to my creative urge when I wrote out these intentions on December 22, 2005. My hope is that you will feel inspired to write your own desires through a statement of your best, even preposterous intentions. You have permission to get "outside the box" and color outside the lines.

My intention is to:

1. Enter into and accept my "savant" status. Perhaps I really was born a genius! At least I know I am different and unique.

2. Live congruently as a creator, continuing the evolution of life. I have my unique and significant style of genius,

and that includes original vision. No one else sees the world through my eyes.

3. Enter the unknown. Imagine the best. Reach for the edges and beyond. Construct a heaven of high vibration, utter safety, and ultimate trust *now*. Create my own "beginners' heaven."

4. Wait, in silence, anticipating what may come—silence of thought and feeling as well as mind.

5. Allow energy to flow into the void. All is here for my awareness and my evolution toward my highest and best Self. I allow it, and I accept it.

6. Stay in the process, without judgment, control, or evaluation.

7. Notice whatever shows up with respect, gentle curiosity, and awe. I will be in the dynamic, fluid, ongoing process of creation.

8. Explore with open-ended questions, anticipating miracles. Miracles are changes in my thoughts, feelings, behaviors, and beliefs. Miracles are always positive.

9. Celebrate the gift through gratitude and awareness. Acknowledge the mystery.

10. Meditate. I will sit comfortably, be still for a few minutes, notice my breathing, allow my thoughts to go on by, and stay in the now moment. In the stillness, I will wait for the next thought, which may just be a creative inspiration.

Intend it. Imagine it. Anticipate it. Allow it. Accept it. Enjoy it. Give thanks for it.

Dreams

Nighttime dreaming is another source of creative inspiration. Keeping a dream journal and working each dream to expose the nuggets of creative possibilities is worth doing. Robert Johnson wrote a book called *Inner Work* in which he describes active imagination and dream understanding. In a workshop with Robert Johnson, he described his own process of rising at 3:00 a.m. and going to his typewriter (this was the era before computers were so easy to use). He put paper in the typewriter in preparation for receiving whatever came. He simply wrote from his own active imagination. His writing might be about his life or it might come from the collective unconscious. It always was of worth. His habit of getting up early to collect whatever his refreshed mind could imagine is a habit worth cultivating.

How can you encourage creativity? What fosters creative inspiration? Where is the muse?

Inspirational Relationships

The most beneficial relationship provides inspiration to get on with becoming one's true self. Inspire is a wonderful word that means to influence, move, or guide by divine or supernatural enspiriting; to exert an animating, enlivening, or exalting influence on; to spur on, impel, motivate. Threats don't necessarily *inspire* people to work. We would do well to pay a handsome salary to any supportive person who provides inspiration for us! The root of the word is spirit, and to be inspired means to be filled with spirit. From the vibrational energy called spirit, we can create.

Close relationships have the power to dampen or warm the creative juices. I would prescribe one for you if I could. My mother, Victoria Kiker McNeely, was one of those positive people who inspired others toward authenticity. I would give you that kind of relationship if I could. My children have provided the stretching experiences that require creative solutions. I confess to many times being reactive rather than creative. I would give you that kind of stretching if I could. The reality is that every relationship is designed to expand our creativity or reduce us to reactivity. The

47

relationship provides the stimulus, and we choose the response. Yes, that is both the good news and the bad news. See chapter 7 for more about positive relationships.

Creative Work Needs "the Silence"

I am amazed how we are in a different era, born out of the technical-industrial age, and how our work is necessarily shifting in its focus because of the transition. For more than two thousand years, we have worked in a hands-on productivity where articles, whether they are articles of clothing or articles of war machinery, were made with physical labor. The factory was a noisy place with little or no time for contemplation or reflection. Farms were family-owned factories of their own sort. I can see Mr. Elam, our blacksmith in our little community, talking with all the people while he heated the iron that he transformed into horseshoes, hammering them out on his anvil. My daddy talked to him while he did his work. Most endeavors in the technical-industrial age were productive work done in a noisy environment. I can see my aunts and my mother sewing dresses, making quilts, cooking, or milking cows, and they could talk or yell at each other with no problem in the production of the things they made or the work they did. We were able to do our work at the same time we talked, sang, or yelled over the noise. Work was a kind where you made something that was tangible. It required physical labor, with a measure of mental work to keep it successful. We are nearing the end of that age, and the balance is more toward mental work with a measure of physical labor to carry out its processes.

Now we have work where we think, where we create ideas, and where imagination is needed, work that is best done with mental contemplation or quiet thinking time. This kind of work means we often cannot touch the product. We can only see its output if it is a good product. I am talking about work that involves strategizing, writing, creating, or conceptualizing. Do we think we can create with a lot of stimuli (voices talking, noisy machinery, bad lighting, uncomfortable temperatures, etc.)? Is creative work possible without specific conditions? Does one size office or workspace fit all as it did in the age of conformity and mass production? Do we need more Walden Ponds to allow us to write or think in solitude?

I talked with someone recently who is an artist. He does his best work late in the night. His neighbor parties and keeps him awake when he wants to be painting in complete solitude. Another person is a business writer, and she is in a multiple-person office where the conversations often are too "chatty" to afford her a train of thought that will help create an inspirational message. A computer expert is expected to produce programs or write code with neighbors on the phone or visitors to the center stopping by to make small talk. A musician tries to write her songs and cannot because there are too many interruptions.

We are emerging from the Piscean Age, where we had pyramids of power with one person on top issuing orders and where the work was still similar to the harvesting of crops or making machines. Now we are entering the age of the individual, the age of ideas, and the age of intuition—the Age of Aquarius. All those are internal concepts. Ideas require time to imagine; creative art needs gestation time; computer science demands long periods of isolation; and writing of any kind demands absolute silence, as well as isolation.

All our institutions are changing, and work itself is in a giant shift. It seems to be moving from noisy to quiet and from hands-on labor to think tank idea generation.

My generation grew up on the farm. Now, urban living is the norm. Remembering farm scenes, I see lots of noise and much hard physical labor. Picking cotton was a picture of community life, with great fun and laughter, lots of singing, whistling, and general camaraderie. The boss was the foreman who weighed the cotton sacks (empty first and then full, subtracting the difference).

All farm work was more fun when the neighbors and all family members shared such things as threshing the grain, killing the hogs, or building a barn. Usually there was a leader who directed the operation. In the same era, factory work was noisy and regulated, with line bosses or shift foremen who kept things moving and met quotas. Schools still operate with a bell ringing when classes change, reflecting factory and mining practices. Schools still ask for silence while "learning" is taking place, but the playground is approved for loud and boisterous activity. I watched a TED talk yesterday where Sir Ken Robinson tells about how schools today are killing creativity. We have a wealth of learning possibilities on the internet and TED is one where you can find rich information delivered in short speeches by experts in many fields. In this particular TED session, Robinson makes the point that we still are operating schools like factories and drugging children to make them conform to an outmoded system. Change is necessary, and we are seeing some school systems meet the challenge when the central teacher "boss" figure becomes more of a group leader-facilitator. Classrooms have more of a quiet buzz signaling the shift. We are caught in the parenthesis between ages. Creative change is imperative.

Honoring Individual Learning Styles

Most of my creative ideas come in the early morning after a night of rest. I usually get up with lots of drive and energy. My thoughts following silent meditation seem to show up the most creative of all. I do my best creating in the mornings. Each individual has different modes of learning and different modes of creative output.

The Aquarian workplace will eventually morph into something that supports individuals who are inventive, creative, innovative, and able to "see" beyond the reality of the day. This remarkable shift will come from honoring individual expressiveness and no longer needing to have the boss of the crew giving orders or keeping score. Engaged employees motivated from within will innovate and create new possibilities in the workplace. Flex-time, project management, people development, and strengths-based cultures are ingredients for future emergence.

There will be a real shift in motivation. When we are able to honor our creativity and our individuality, we will be drawn and not driven. We will be inspired and not controlled. We will come into our own as creative individual "god-seeds," just as Meister Eckhart predicted back in the middle ages. He said that pear trees grow from pear seeds and that humans are "god-seeds." That means we are creators.

In this Aquarian age, we will become God knows what!

Emotional Honesty

Awareness of emotional flow is helpful if you are seeking to unleash your creative juices. Negative emotion hampers creativity. Positive emotion seems to turn on the flow. I discovered the reality that emotions are a great guidance system. When I am feeling down or any other form of negative feeling, I am off track in my purpose in life. When I am on track, I am always in a positive state of feelings. Happiness is a choice.

I recently created lists of negative emotion with the antidote for shifting that emotion. Does this mean that deeply depressed (clinically depressed) individuals can just snap out of it? They cannot without a lot of self-discovery, self-awareness, and self-responsibility. I recall Johnny May (not her real name), who was depressed for years. Her psychiatrist actually administered shock treatments, and she received many psychotropic drugs for her depression. She entered into a form of cognitive (thought) therapy, and through diligent hard work, she became "mercilessly self-aware" that her own thoughts and beliefs were at the root of her deep depression. She did not change overnight, but over the course of years, she valiantly assumed self-responsibility and self-ownership. She re-parented herself. She has become a successfully happy person. We laughed together when she told me that she could not even work up a good hypo-glycemic attack now.

Post-traumatic stress disorder (PTSD) is one diagnosis when a person has suffered drastic trauma, such as war, floods, or sudden injuries. PTSD is the negative aftermath to such awful happenings. Martin Seligman, in his book *Flourish*, describes PTG, which means post-traumatic growth. In PTG, the individual can be helped to find the resilience and strength of character to creatively shift from a limited life into an expanded life. One soldier who returned from Iraq with full-blown PTSD was brought, without drugs, into positive and creative life where she found her destiny through creative service to returning troops.

Some of the world's greatest artists have produced their most creative work out of deep depression. Anger, sadness, guilt, shame, and all negative emotions can be the springboard for expression of the angst of our human condition. Does great creativity spring from great suffering? And does the creative work relieve the suffering? What inspires great creativity? I would like to have a conversation with you and explore these ideas together … creatively.

None of us are victims. None of us are persecutors, nor are we rescuers. These are phony game roles, and we can stop playing neurotic games. You can be sure you are playing a psychological game when the outcome is bad feelings. Joyful feelings are the indicator that no games are being played. Each of us has the power to create the flow of our life. We are the designers of our life story. The past is stored in our memory bank, and that memory bank is an anthology of the stories we have built around our memories. We interpret the story, creating the thoughts and feelings that follow. That story can be a marvelous novel, better than fiction. It can be a comedy, a tragedy, a saga, or a soap opera. We create the story. We write and speak the lines. We stage the play, and we are ultimately the owner of the production. Our story is our greatest creative venture. We can change the story.

All other creative products are the results of the story. You are the creator of the story, and you can join the triple A—becoming the author, actor, and audience in your own life story. That is the challenge as well as the opportunity.

Creativity Requires Dedicated Action

We have learned about the law of attraction in the last few years. I think it could be expressed as the awe of action. Without dedicated behavior aimed at bringing the creative product forth, there will only be the dream. This seems so apparent, and yet I am prone to wait for someone to discover me and hand me a contract on a silver platter, announcing that I am worthy of being a creative person. When I dream up an idea, it remains in idea form until I *do* something. In the doing, the creativity is accomplished.

Procrastination can be a block to creativity. It can be a sign that you are following one of the drivers. Maybe the belief is that as long as you don't risk producing something, you cannot risk failure. You can overcome your tendency to procrastinate by saying, "I can, I will, and I will do it right away."

Right Conditions

Perhaps you have been waiting for inspiration or the right conditions before you can express your creativity. I have known many women who have expanded the meaning and use of creativity. Most of them are teachers of some sort. As I learned from them, these are a summary of what they taught me:

- We are more creative when we go into the process without expectation.
- Accept yourself as a highly creative expression of the divine.

- Create a space of safety, high vibration, and respect for the unknown.
- Invite whatever you perceive as the muse, your creative spirit.
- Relax and wait without interfering.
- Respect whatever comes, yet be willing to allow evolution as the process continues.
- Sometimes questions come. It is best not to force the answers. Just wait.
- Feel gratitude for your power to create.
- Accept your own stream of consciousness.

You have a perfect *right* to be creative. You have the *responsibility* to learn what it takes to create. Once you have gained the skills and knowledge to make something—a painting, a piece of art, a design for anything, writing, projects, ideas, a political design, any aha moments—then you are free to mentally *rehearse* your finished product in your imagination. Seeing it to its fruition will ensure that it will happen. You can *relax* and allow the time it takes to bring your creation to fruition. Then you can celebrate and *reap your reward, rejoicing* in your innovative contribution. Dream as big as you can. See, hear, and feel the highest and best future that wants to emerge. Stepping up to your leadership possibilities as one woman will be easier because you are now transforming the future through the joy of your own creative imagination.

CHAPTER 4:

Grow Up

The Joy of Evolving

Preparation: Facing the northeast, imagine yourself going to the farthest reaches in space and visiting a star. The star is Altair, the beginning of the Aquarian Age. Look back at planet Earth in the Milky Way galaxy, our little island home. Let your thoughts reveal your destiny on that island. The color is green. Follow your imagination as you allow your heart center to fully expand, Aphrodite style, into the quintessential Possible Woman. The Greek goddess Aphrodite is the archetype to consider. She represents things of the heart. The heart center is the pivot from which women's wisdom and women's action flow. Think what this statement means to you.

One Woman Growing Up:
a Sampling from *My Spiritual Memories*

I don't remember when I first felt the deep, stomach-aching fear, but the first thirty years of my life, I existed in a state of anxiety stemming from the thought that I wasn't "saved." I believed my thoughts.

The beginnings of the fear were subtle, entangled with my childhood interactions with the gods of my life: my family and the preachers. One day during the loud and long sermon in our little country church, I wiped my runny nose on my dress because I didn't have a handkerchief. It was 1934. We were in the midst of the Great Depression, and my dress was a treasure made over from my mother's wedding dress. Understandably, when we arrived home, she scolded me for ruining my dress. I felt sick, tinged with feelings of rejection from my mother and the "hell-fire and damnation" judgment by the preacher. That was one incident among many that built the layers of fear deep in my psyche. I created a belief that consumed me: I was not enough. Looking back, I can see that all of my psychotherapeutic growth has been around that self-belief, "I am not enough, and I will never be enough."

My deepest fear was of the rapture. I was six years old when a Methodist evangelist illustrated his sermons with paintings of people who were left behind at the rapture. There was a man with a coal oil lamp looking through his house for his family, but Jesus had come and he was the only one not saved. They had gone to live with Jesus, and the man was utterly lost and alone.

So I feared that I would be alone, which is separation anxiety of the worst sort. Even after I walked the aisle to ask for salvation, I still had the fear. I was not enough, and I was utterly alone. Finally, a turning point came in the middle of the night. I couldn't sleep for fear that Jesus would return as promised, any minute, day or night, and they would be taken but I would not be included. I ached all over. The fear suffocated me beyond my endurance. I got up from my bed, walked on the cold linoleum to my parents' bed, and woke them to confess that I was afraid I wasn't saved. This required an enormous leap of faith for me. I shared what I was feeling.

My mother told me it was their fault since they didn't read the Bible enough and have a family altar. The rest is a blur: the fear remained, but now I knew I couldn't discuss it with my parents because they would blame themselves, heaping guilt upon guilt. (I think this was the moment I chose to become a born-again rescuer.) I believed, "I am not enough, I am alone, but the way out is to be very, very good." I was twelve years old when I heard a preacher predict the return of Jesus on a certain date, based on his study of Revelation. I listened very carefully and calculated that I would be twenty-two years old when Jesus returned. Sure enough, when I was twenty-one years old, I attended a revival meeting, and the preacher said that many people weren't saved because their baptism was wrong. By his reasoning, I had been baptized too soon and didn't really know what I was doing. That was why I still wasn't saved. It made sense to me and seemed to be a way out of the fear, so I walked the aisle and got baptized again, this time in a real baptistry. I told my husband the whole long story, and he assured me that I was saved.

Finally, the fear abated somewhat. But then my husband died. I associated his death with my unworthiness. After all, didn't God bless those who were saved? Didn't God answer prayer? I had prayed, believing, and still my husband died. My goodness and my actions were still not enough.

So God died too.

From this state of being asleep, my consciousness began to expand. I began to learn. I studied psychology. I studied theology. I studied philosophy. I studied everything that would give me a measure of human understanding. I asked why I existed, what purpose I served on earth. I concluded that most of what I had believed was manmade, right along with guilt and shame and fear.

My perception of God changed. My concept of soul and consciousness was stretched. I realized that the world of my childhood didn't make room for females in the high holy places. I had excluded myself from holiness because I was a woman, a girl child. God was male. The preachers were male; the church leaders were male. I began to wake up to the reality of my self-image, perceptions, and projections. I probably believed that women were okay only if they served with sweetness, long-suffering, and smiles. My thoughts created the angst of my life, and I believed my thoughts. I created those thoughts, and I can change those thoughts.

Maybe all those years of oppressive religious dogma are just that—in the past. Each one of us has the privilege of examining our beliefs. Were they inculcated from a time of dependency? If they are adopted without scrutiny, they are imposed from outside us. Growth requires awakening to our beliefs, which lead to our thinking, feeling, and doing. Today, my new belief is that life is to be enjoyed, not just endured. I further believe that any one of us can create a lifelong compass of joy.

You are not finished yet! You have more expansion waiting. You are growing, changing, maturing, evolving, and realizing that life is all about turning points and change. Consciousness evolves in a spiral, ever widening and expanding.

Yes, growing up is hard to do. Wisdom is born of pain, says Helen Reddy, in her song "I Am Woman." The lesson for me has been to get beyond my victim status, into my sense of being my own woman, with my own beliefs, thoughts, feelings, and behaviors. That means that every choice I make is not a "have to" or "should" but a true choice—will or won't—and it is made by me. I want those choices to be made from my highest Self, the one that is in alignment with my purpose in life.

Finding My Calling

Who did I come here to be? Why am I alive at this time? My purpose in life, this calling, cannot feel like martyrdom or stagnation. It is the ultimate engagement. It will be based in deep desire, with action taken because of curiosity, drive, motivation, or that still, small voice that we have inside guiding and sometimes goading us.

I remember studying angels, and my helper-therapist who was psychic told me I had eleven angel guides. I wondered why they never called, never wrote, and didn't seem to reach out. She said that they speak through your intuition. I was so practical that I couldn't decide when it was intuition and when it was ego that was speaking to me. Then, another very intuitive therapist told me that I would enjoy what I was doing if I followed my calling. That made sense. I enjoyed being a marriage and family therapist. I especially enjoyed helping people move toward real potential and achievements that were out of their range of thinking when they first came in for a counseling session. I relished those moments when a good person moved on to being better and then to excellent. I didn't enjoy the "stuckness" of those who could be labeled dysfunctional. I was kind and caring, I listened, I modeled what I wanted them to know, and I taught them new skills, offered them new knowledge. I rejoiced as they improved and found their way. I came to understand that their way was the right way for them, just as parents are brought to that humbled state of realization that each child is an individual who has the *right* to write his or her own story.

In all the years of working as a counselor-therapist, one strong impression kept recurring: people really don't change very much. Since I was acting as a change agent and my impression was that they couldn't or wouldn't change, then perhaps I was not following my calling. Change was the central subject, and I had much to learn about it.

I have changed a lot in these thirty-odd years of working as a "shrink" and an agent of change. I now think of myself as an expander instead of being the traditional shrink. What I have learned and what I really believe is that since people don't change that much, I will do best to find out what their talents are, help them accept those talents, and move with them into expansion of those talents through more skills, insights, realizations, and knowledge. Self-acceptance is a big key in this growing-up process. Self-acceptance, self-forgiveness, and self-love are necessary if we as women are to give up our Cinderella conspiracies, our martyr complexes, and evolve into twenty-first-century possibilities for women. Our future is being created by us human beings at the same time we are living it out. Women are half of that constructive force. We can partner with men in the creation of our future life on planet Earth. I am optimistic about our future.

The theories of Ilia Prigogine give me great hope. Prigogine won a Nobel Prize for his theory of dissipative structures, in which he said that old structures dissipate and are replaced with new ones, expanding the old. His theory is a bridge from science to social systems. My work with family systems revealed that the goal of a family system is to self-destruct. The family grows outward into the community, and each child establishes his or her own family. The old structure dissipates, and the new structure builds on the heritage from the past. That is the evolutionary journey of our human race. And that is the one-woman journey for each individual woman. Whatever comes to us is helpful in that it stretches us beyond where we were before. We cannot deny the wisdom that is learned from mistakes, conflicts, challenges, and tragic circumstances. Just as scar tissue is stronger than undamaged tissue, so we are shaped and strengthened by our interactions with the outside world.

This requires a big shift in perception. I was taught as a little girl that God is love. As a marriage therapist, I learned that our chief challenge is to learn how to love. Growing up meant, for me, examining all old beliefs that had been inculcated by my culture. Expanding into new thoughts about science and spirituality has been a quest for me in my adult life. Psychology, biology, and theology hold my curiosity in high and positive excitement. Psychology means the study of the soul, biology is the study of living organisms, and theology is the collective wisdom from our earliest human experience—trying to make sense of life and our existence. Each woman will do well to pursue her own learning about the deep meaning of her life. She will step up with surety when she knows what she believes. I offer some of what I have come to believe, hoping that you will be challenged and inspired to do the same.

I see our human condition as one that rumbles, stumbles, and bumbles into its future. We are driven to survive. We are inspired to thrive. We are creating as we go along. We just might reach a tipping point and all of us shift into the delicious realization that we are living expressions of whatever we think of as a higher order, and that is good.

Joy is our birthright. This book is about our lifelong compass of joy. When any one woman gets into her joy, she is transformed. Inevitably, she looks around at the world she is in and becomes a leader in taking that world into her version of heaven on earth. These are words that convey the reality of a benevolent life force. War and suffering are human-made—the collective shadow of the generations gone before. Violence is one of the least-effective means of change. War is not a technique that brings peace. Imprisonment and punishment are glaring failures in the mission of changing humans for the better. We would be better by now if all those methods worked!

The year was 1984, Orwellian, life-changing, and it was the year I decided to work with women. There were reasons for that choice. First, most of my psychotherapy practice was made up of women. Second, I was a woman, and my life growth process was a personal story lived by one woman—me. Third, the need for women to move beyond their relegated lot in life was imperative. And fourth, we were entering the Aquarian Age, which seemed to me to be made for women. The thrill comes when one woman reaches for and explores her own authenticity as a unique and significant individual human being. My purpose in life has been solidified. I know what I came here to do. I came to the planet Earth for a lifetime of service to the evolutionary development of women. Women are born leaders, ready for the Aquarian Age.

I want you to know the story of how my purpose evolved over the years. Looking back, I can see the beginning seed, which has become a concept I called the Possible Woman. Please enjoy my story of the birth of the Possible Woman concept:

One of my clients was a fast-talking, hyper-acting young man who taught in a local college. He came to me so he could work with his life story and especially on his failed relationships with women. He was a devotee of *The Power of Positive Thinking* by Norman Vincent Peale. In his therapy, he imagined himself in a successful endeavor where he would make a great deal of money. He read Napoleon Hill's book, *Think and Grow Rich* and was inventing a manifestation for wealth and success. The story evolved into his renting a large auditorium in a distant city for a one-night lecture. He was going to sell tickets for $10 a person and fill the thousand-seat hall, thereby earning ten thousand dollars in one hour, which was a vast improvement over his college instructor's salary. He asked me to introduce him, and I agreed. I should add that he hired a publicity team, and it did seem plausible with a media blitz that he might have a large crowd in attendance. I tell you this story to let you know how I started my work with women.

The night of the lecture, I gathered up three women friend-clients to ride with me to this inspired marketing event where the handsome young man was going to get rich quick. Coincidentally, the car broke down on the way, and I was not able to introduce him to his audience. It seems serendipitous that the catalytic converter was the reason for the breakdown. None of us were aware of a major turning point at the time.

The Possible Woman®

The hidden outcome was that we four women planned a really nice seminar on "Becoming Your Best Self," and it was a great success. This was the launch of our Possible Woman® seminars, the cruises, the spa retreats, and the eventual business events of major proportions. One of those four women was Linda Wind, and she has expressed her mission for women's leadership development through her corporation, Wind Enterprises®. Linda's contribution to the growth of women's leadership has touched thousands of women. Twenty years later, she hosts large Possible Woman® events in Atlanta, Georgia, with well-known keynote speakers and great breakout sessions led by women entrepreneurs. Women use these events for growth and development. Businesses send women to these events for the purpose of helping them move into leadership positions. A scholarship program has evolved into a large enterprise helping women who are aspiring to go back to school. The success stories are abundant and full of optimistic future possibilities. We asked two questions at these conferences: "Who are you?" and "What can you be?" I invite you to answer those two questions from your own whole-hearted mind. The time has come in which women will move into leadership on this fragile planet Earth. You are the possible woman who can assume your individual leadership role.

I am eternally grateful for that young college teacher who had a wild dream that precipitated our dreams. His story is also fascinating and would make a bestselling book.

Stages of Growth, According to the Spiral of Consciousness

One of my pneumonic devices described earlier is the clock of awareness, where I ask you to think about your beliefs, thoughts, feelings, and behavior and get the connectedness between these four mental constructs.

Another device is "The Spiral of Consciousness," where I look at human growth and development as turns of an ever-heightening, ever-broadening spiral. I labeled these with words, all beginning with the letter A. Picture a spiral that moves upward from asleep to aware to awake to alive to attracting to allowing to authenticity—seven rounds of growth. These are also development of individual talents. As we add skills and knowledge, we move upward and outward.

The Spiral of Consciousness

Asleep

My experience with people is that the majority still believes that the cause of unhappiness comes from the outside. We are prone to believe that what happened has been caused by someone else or circumstances beyond our control. The thoughts reveal the belief because they are reactionary instead of creative. Everything seems to take place because of something else. There is a constant vigilance about what causes feelings of either love or fear. The results are identity confusion, feelings of being separate, alone, afraid, ashamed, guilty, and inadequate.

Recently, I worked with a woman, the president of her own corporation, who brought a current problem to our session. Her partner had misrepresented the company to a prospective customer, and she was upset. She spent the session describing in detail how the partner was in error. She spoke eloquently about her own credentials and experience and how she would never do such things. When I asked what she was feeling, she spoke of being sick with rage. Her belief was that the partner had caused the rage.

She also spoke of her fear for the success of their enterprise unless her partner changed her behavior. When we discussed the partner's strengths and the contribution she brought to the business, the president decided that she would do relationship work with her partner in a later session.

In this trance, which I labeled the *asleep* state, we believe that our experience is determined by outside persons and events. We operate from a common belief that we are separate. In the trance, we cannot perceive that we are part of life, that we are one with everything. We are alone. Life seems a battle or, at best, a struggle. Vigilance is the norm. Our thoughts are reactionary, and feelings follow in accord with thinking and believing. Dichotomous thinking means we have either/or concepts instead of both/and oneness. Our emotional flow will tend to go the path of love or the path of fear. Love means we live in the belief that we are part of the whole. Fear means we think we are alone. Our behavior will be alert and vigilant, with many interpretations of others and events. The path of fear and separateness is revealed when something happens, and the response is made with blame, judgment, criticism, or faultfinding. Arguments with defensiveness follow. Each person seems to want to prove that he or she is the innocent victim in the circumstance. Nothing will change until the players begin to be aware.

Aware

We are possibly the only species on our planet who are capable of self-reflection through self-awareness. *Awareness* is the door to growth, and it is accomplished when we pay attention to what our senses are telling us. To be aware is to be in the now moment. A simple awareness exercise is to stop what you are doing and focus on what you are seeing, hearing, tasting, touching, or smelling. Breathe deeply, and ponder the meaning you are giving to each of these outside forces. Be aware of your thoughts. Notice how you place meaning on what you see and hear. Notice your judgments about how your tastes or smells are good or bad. Notice how you are interpreting what you touch or what touches you. If you simply let yourself be aware with no urge to do anything, you will begin the spiral toward your self-realization. Remember that self-realization, the growth of your consciousness, is a good thing. It begins with a belief that experience is generated from the inside. Thoughts that are curious and investigative are part of your awareness. Feelings are important guidance tools. If you feel good, you are on track in your self-discovery. If you feel bad, you are moving more into the downward spiral and reverting to the belief that your reality comes from the outside. Your behavior is what you say and do in your words, tone of voice, facial expression, body postures, and gestures. In this turn of the spiral of consciousness, your behavior will be observing, intuiting, and noticing what you are thinking and deliberately choosing to be more aware than anxious. Awareness is the door to realization that we are all one and we are a part of the whole. Self-awareness of score-keeping and benevolent observation of the need to control are possible and worth doing. All the defenses and attacks can be seen with a tolerant kind of self-forgiveness. The upward spiral starts with hope and optimism. Self awareness, self-acceptance and discovery of the life patterns we live will allow the possibility of moving toward the next turn of the spiral.

Awake

In this turn of the spiral, we begin to take away the cobwebs from our programmed mind. *Awake* is more like realizing that I do generate my own experience by my reactions. My survival reactions are all part of a trance-like asleep state in which I am really unaware of life in its fullest form. I long to be deep awake instead of deep asleep. I investigate how I learned these habits of behavior. Most were learned when I was still dependent on others. I came to believe in their version of me. I can now take charge of that belief and grasp the truth that I generate my own experience. I can focus my thoughts on learning more about my past habits and how I have survived up to now through some of those defense mechanisms. My feelings are like the gas gauge on my car. Full means I have positive feelings, and empty means I have drained my container and am functioning now from the flow of stressful, old, and negative feelings. The good news is that I can change the negative feeling. I can discover the power of thoughts to change feelings. My behavior will be more like going with the Flow. The upward spiral brings this deep awake feeling of seeing the world through fresh eyes and being responsive to every stimulus that comes to us with ownership and responsibility for what we are creating. Living in this awake state means more laughter, more love, and more light. It means more enthusiasm for learning, working, and playing. It means physical, mental, and spiritual ownership.

Alive

This state of aliveness is anchored in a new belief in my oneness and connectedness with all life. When I am functioning from this turn of the spiral, I have thoughts that sound more curious, with awe and wonder emerging as my new state of mind. I feel the energy of my own volition, and I am in a state of forward motion with full participation, even enthusiasm. If I move downward, my feelings will signal that I am avoiding or denying my consciousness. Tuning out, giving up, and not being engaged are signals that I am drifting into my downward spiral. I can return with the magic of awareness. Awareness of feelings is the most beneficial skill we can learn. To know what sensations our body is experiencing is to know the feeling flow. I repeat the rule: positive emotion is the sign that we are spiraling upward.

I teach from a wonderful little book, *How Full Is Your Bucket?* by Tom Rath and Donald O. Clifton. In that book, the behavior of the upward spiral into positive growth and development is made very clear. As Don Clifton taught, we are all given an invisible bucket that holds our positive emotion as well as an invisible dipper. The theory of the dipper and the bucket says that we cannot fill our bucket by dipping out of someone else's bucket. In fact, when we dip or fill, our own bucket is being affected. Dipping from others' or our own bucket causes us to spiral downward; filling buckets will increase our positive flow. The only way we fill our own bucket is to fill other buckets. The principles from the book are also worth learning and following. They are good thoughts and beliefs to incorporate on your way to your authenticity. These five principles are: 1) Help prevent bucket dipping; 2) Shine a light on what is right; 3) Give unexpectedly; 4) Make best friends; and 5) a twist on the Golden Rule—do unto others as *they* would like to be done unto. The new version of the Golden Rule means we can get to know other people and learn what they like. For me, these five principles help in becoming fully human and fully *alive*. Being in the *alive* turn of the spiral takes us into relationships with hope, self-responsibility, and never-ending generosity. The magic of the dipper and bucket theory is that when we fill the buckets of other people, our own bucket fills up—from a never-ending supply.

Attracting

Now we get to the good stuff. When we are aware, awake, and alive, we can exercise the real magic of being human, and that magic is that we do attract what we think about. This turn of the spiral is fixed in a new belief, which says that I attract good or bad into my world, I can take responsibility for everything that happens to me, and I can ask forgiveness for my species. We are still evolving. We are where we are in our journey of evolutionary life. We are love in ultimate expression. We can be grateful, and we can love. Believing that we are therefore good and that we have the power to attract more good will lead to thoughts that are exploratory into learning about love. Loving one another may not be easy, yet it can be done.

The law of attraction has received great notice recently. I have experienced the truth of this law, mostly in the negative sense. What I think about, negatively or positively, really does happen in my world. If it feels bad and the thoughts are negative, it is being created. If it feels good and the thoughts are positive, it is being created. It is what it is. Our interpretation gives us the experience of the "it." The big truth is that all these "its" are "I." Any impersonal pronoun can be interpreted as self-expression. If you will listen to your words and be aware that words are symbols that describe us, you can discover how your own law of attraction is in action. The real lesson from this turn of the upward spiral is that what we think about does tend to come about. This is also true in the downward spiral: negative thoughts attract, like magnets with iron filings, actions that are like the thoughts.

Allowing

When I create through my thoughts, I will experience what I made up. How I receive what I have created is my next turn of the spiral. I can allow or receive the good or the bad. I believe that I am part of life on the planet Earth for a brief period of chronological time. I accept life and contribute my energy to bettering life. My thoughts will be knowledge-seeking thoughts. I am drawn to find my truth, my way. I like the saying that happiness is the way, not that we are finding our way to happiness. My thinking is drawn to the silence of meditation. I am glad to have time to ponder and wonder. My feelings are more in the present moment with an open mind, open heart, and open will. Openness to life is the way of receiving what is. My actions are more calm, cool, collected, and communicative. I am caring, curious, and interested in what goes on. This turn of the spiral means accepting what is and living in the now with exploratory curiosity.

Authentic

I have moments of being real. I am sometimes very genuine. I relish the belief that I create the dream I am living. I believe that happiness is my choice. I further believe that joy is my natural state. My thoughts are aligned with my life purpose. I hope you have moments like this, too. There is an essence of soul being eternal with mind-body-spirit one with the greatcreative life force. My feelings are still guiding me. My behavior is congruent, integrated, purposeful, and joyful. I am all "lined up" with my very best possibility. Not easy to do, but what are we here for anyway if not to become who we truly are? When we have reached our true self, even for a short moment, there is a feeling of being one with all. There is a radiant generosity toward all expressions of life. Like a spiral that extends upward, ever widening, we are shining our light. The upward spiral is eternally growing, shining, joining, and genuine. From *authenticity* we become open to life and open to love. The unique individual self can express creativity, genuineness, intentionality, choice, flow, vision, peace, hope, joy, forgiveness, compassion, empathy, warmth, and understanding. Our entelechy is expressed. Entelechy is a Greek word that means our dynamic purposiveness, our complete authenticity.

The Downward Spiral

If the spiral goes upward toward our true selves, then perhaps it goes downward to our false self. Using again the A words: down from asleep to attached instead of aware, to vigilantly anxious instead of awake, to afraid, avoiding, and ashamed instead of alive, to attracting negative results instead of positive outcomes, to allowing or accepting our reduced status as human beings instead of allowing all that is good to come to us, to living in an adapted false self instead of true authenticity. The corresponding thoughts, feelings, and behavior represent the path of fear.

Attachment theory means that we have invented a story with meaning about an event or happening, and we believe our story. I remember a client who was certain that her dentist was negligent in not reminding her to get her teeth cleaned. When she developed gum problems, she became "attached" to her story that it was the dentist's fault. We cannot be aware of our power until we tell a different story—one where we are responsible for our own behavior.

Vigilant and anxious sensations are felt in the pit of the stomach as a constant alert state based in fear. Our moments are taken in and reacted to with judgment and serious demeanor. There is an alert vigilance in every encounter. Worry is the normal state of mind. Constant vigilance requires a lot of energy, which leaves us in a state of distress, anxiety, and living on the edge of some dreaded possibility.

Afraid is full-blown fear in action. Our body responses, learned in our ancient evolutionary history, assess every eventuality as a time to make ready to fight, flee, or freeze. The feeling permeates all the tissue of our body as we gear up to resist, run away, or get very small and invisible. The general belief is that life is a constant threat to existence itself, so we avoid adventure or risk, we live in fear, and at the root of it all, we are ashamed, fearing we are not enough. Avoidance is an extension of the fear through denial, repression, or suppression. Rooted in a basic self-picture of unworthiness akin to shame, the fear lurks at every turn of the downward spiral. We are not really alive but in a trance of old habit patterns.

So we attract the very thing that we dread. Like unto itself is drawn. Automatic behavior based in learned habit patterns is the downward opposite of attracting what we want. We are automatons functioning in daily desperation and believing that life is what it is. Pure happiness and satisfaction are not in the picture of life as we live it in this level of the downward spiral. We say that other people or circumstances cause our suffering and live out our lives in reaction to what is on the outside instead of creating a life of authenticity.

We accept our bad luck, our fate, and continue following the negative turn of the spiral. Allowing means in this turn of the spiral that things happen to us without our volition or generation. Life affects us. We are not in charge of life. We are not allowing the good things of life because we are immersed in the belief that life happens to us, and we don't have much real power to affect life and create it as we desire.

At the nadir of the downward spiral, we are living in an adaptive state of being. We have adapted to all the outside circumstances and are driven to please, be perfect, be strong, be careful, try hard, and hurry up. The probability of being on drugs of some kind is high. In the downward spiral, our physical body begins to reflect the script through pain, dis-ease, and angst. We have reliable research showing us that our psychological events actually do influence our neural brain patterns, which really do influence our own immune system events. At the bottom of the downward spiral, we are the living version of a "false self" and we experience the results of inauthenticity.

Born Free

The more conscious we are, the more freedom we experience. We learn to be free from our culturally imposed state of socialization. Becoming conscious of our own patterns of thoughts, feelings, and behavior, noticing our instinctual urges, and examining our cultural conditioning are three prime requisites to being free. We have power, and our power exists in the microsecond of time between stimulus and response. We are free to choose our responses. We are always free to choose our thoughts. Possibilities expand as our thoughts help us wake up. The most adventurous thought of all is that we are one with all life, yet we are in the individual experience of being separate. Being conscious allows us to express and experience in the ever-upward, ever-outward spiral of consciousness. The spiral of growth pulls us into the future with deep awareness.

There exists the need for us humans to begin to take charge of our lives. Each individual is unique and very significant. My program in the 1980s on KLUX radio in Corpus Christi, Texas, was called "Taking Charge." It can begin when we get some glimmer that we are a person of power. We have ownership of our beliefs, thoughts, feelings, and behavior, which is real power. We have choices in what we believe about ourselves, others, and the world. We can take charge of cognition and think different thoughts. Feelings follow thoughts and beliefs. Responsible behavior is really a choice.

When you let go of fear, you will cultivate love and forgiveness. Letting go of the need to judge will result in more compassion and caring. And when you let go of blaming, you are free to manifest great possibilities. Your feelings will be authentic and serve as signals to guide you. You can get beyond the old, automatic story adapted for survival purposes. You can acknowledge and feel enthusiasm because you will have healed the pain-body. Then you will be on your path to authenticity. Instead of just surviving, you actually can begin thriving.

This whole book is about you as a woman taking charge of your life story and creating yourself the way you choose. At age eighty-two and counting, I am still growing into the person I came here to be. I am conscious of my leadership, and I challenge you to wake up to your own leadership. You are the Possible Woman, growing up, maturing, evolving, and stepping up to your possibilities as the unique and significant human being you were born to be.

CHAPTER 5:

Lighten Up

The Joy of Play

Preparation: Face the west and ponder about playing. The star is Arcturus, which holds meaning about the ancient ones. I think of older people who have discovered the futility of being serious. They lighten up as they age. They take off the mask and are more able to be in the moment. Playing games, dancing, or playing music is a part of the wisdom of aging. Think about your life and what you can do to increase your joy of play. The color is blue like the sky on a clear day. The mythological figure is Hera, the wife or great mate. Remember all your playful relationships, and imagine even more playfulness in your life.

Playing Music

Playing music is one of my lifelong joys. Music helps me lighten up. I remember the day I added music to my list of health principles. My husband Paul and I were driving to a meeting. Neither one of us were in a mood to attend this event. My body was exhausted, and my mind was tired and burnt out. Paul's week had been stressful, and he also was less than enthusiastic. My head burned, my eyes were dull, and my conversation had degenerated to grunts and groans. My throat was getting scratchy, and my body was sending me flu-like symptoms. True to our habit of being dependable, we pressed on, taking our bodies for granted without much awareness or regard. In an attempt to help, I searched for a tape to play on the car stereo system. I chose Don Campbell's audiocassette tape entitled, "Heal Yourself with Your Own Voice." We began to listen and to follow Don's instructions for toning. He told us to use our voice to "tone" the vowels. Paul joined me in a loving act of support for my caterwauling.

There we were, driving down the highway at seventy miles an hour, howling *"AAAAAAAA-EEEEEEE-IIIIIIII-OOOOOO-UUUUUUUU,"* and we began to laugh. We continued through the entire tape, following instructions to the letter. Fifty miles down the road, to my amazement, my energy returned full strength. Paul reported the same effect. Our mood had shifted toward positive, but more than that, a mysterious shift had taken place in my physical feelings. My throat didn't feel sore, my flu symptoms were gone, my head had cleared, and my body felt great. We were both transformed into the prime of good, healthy bodies, minds, and spirits. We were into a special new kind of intimacy. We had changed in a profound way. The results were that we actually enjoyed the meeting. We drove home in a nice, mellowed-out state. In addition, the power of the effect lasted several days.

This event is one of many illustrations of the true power of music. Music changes our mood. There is growing evidence that music provides healing. Whether we play music in some band, make our own music, or simply listen to music, there is an effect on our mental, emotional, spiritual, and physical health.

In my mother's family, music was our best style of communing. Each of the six Kiker children played an instrument. Grandma Kiker would wash the dishes after their meals, and her instructions to her children were, "Now you children know what you must do."

This meant that they were to entertain her while she did the work of washing the dishes by playing music for her. And so it was that when we attended family reunions, each grandchild was expected to play something. We didn't sit around and visit verbally. We made music, and our communication was melodic, rhythmic, and very loving. It was our way of belonging. We played together in other ways too. Lively games of Hide and Seek, Blind Man's Bluff, and London Bridge were part of our togetherness. Music was the glue that bound us in family harmony. To this day, I feel good when I go to a home and see a piano there. That home seems impoverished to me if musical instruments are absent. Music is in my very bones, my DNA, and my life and is vital to my health. While it seems a mystery, I can personally attest to the power of playing music. Music is my best style of play.

Perhaps we can be productive leaders even as we have fun. Can we admit that the human path includes playfulness, joy, laughter, and pure fun?

A Play Day

My friend and I ran away yesterday. We lightened up. Some say that angels fly because they know how to lighten up! We left our daily world where schedules, goals, habits, and productivity were ruling us. We said, "For a few hours, we are going to do only what we want to do." Each of us had some ideas about that. Those ideas came forth in spurts of impish and rebellious plans. We were into a flow of being reactive and counterproductive, meaning we were just determined not to do what we *ought* to do that day. Perhaps rebellion is the necessity to "prime the pump" of our flow in the world. Once we got past the reactive, rebellious ideas of stopping the world, since we wanted to get off, we were in a state of high glee.

If you analyze the process of doing what it takes to have a vacation, a period of fun, or a day of play, and you discover that you have such an internal task driver that you have to rebel to get to the play day, then the next thing is to recognize your true freedom. You really don't have to justify playing. Nature teaches us that. The most creative acts of nature come when there is a messy playfulness. The most inventive minds come forth with genius-level creations through a trial-and-error process, very much akin to the play in which children are absorbed. This is the area of life where we can learn to lighten up.

My friend and I took our day. It was a totally unscheduled day, in which we celebrated ourselves as the lighthearted, playful human beings we can be. It was a delicious respite from the daily grind. My response was to work easily and with joy after the refreshing break. It seemed that I got more done in a shorter time. I was more efficient, and my mind was more alert.

Looking in the dictionary for the meaning of the word, I discovered ninety-four meanings for play. I "play is a state of being that is pleasurable." Play energizes us, enlivens us, eases our burdens, and renews our natural optimism. Play means fun, zest, freedom of movement, and absorption in the moment. Play is correlated to success and is often self-directed. Play restores us to sanity, encourages our creativity, reduces our stress, and carries us to that place of utter beingness where time stands still and all is now. The flow defined by Mihaly Csikszentmihalyi in his book *Flow* is a mental state where we are intensely immersed in a feeling of energized focus. We are engaged, we are involved, and the activity is all-consuming. It is completely focused motivation. It is the opposite of the stultifying feelings of depression and the agitation of free-floating anxiety. Flow is like spontaneous joy and is very much akin to play as I am using it here. Real engagement is being in the flow. It feels like high play.

Engagement Is High Play

Play may be the most important part of this whole book. We knew the value and pursuit of play as children, and we have either forgotten or we have had it overlain with responsibility. We have relegated play to the realm of children and taken it out of our world as working grown-ups. Yet engagement is a quality we desire in our work force. Engagement means absorption, it means getting to do what we do best, and it means that we have someone who calls forth our best talents. When we watch children on the playground, we see leaders who know how to arrange all the various talented individuals so that their team wins. We see managers who seem to know just who needs encouragement, who needs to be drawn out, and who needs a friend. We confuse maturity with seriousness and certainty of beliefs. Child play is more in the nature of exploration and adventure. It includes lots of laughter and explosive shouting or impulsive poking, pushing, or prodding. Things are funny even when jokes are not. Smiles, laughter, tears, spontaneity, and non-self-conscious behavior are part of the playfulness of children. Somehow we grew up believing that all those wondrous, exciting moments must be put aside if we were to be acceptable grownups.

Females get different messages about being grown up. Generational beliefs still are the causative factor in how we women of certain ages behave. Maybe we dare hope that we can lighten up enough to bring back the joys of being little girls. As joyful women, we have a creative contribution to make to our society, our world, and the future of all generations.

Women as leaders can bring this element of high play into the flow of life on this planet. The absorption of the mind into a task, as a child playing in a park or sandbox, compares to a leader who is completely engaged in the task at hand. The friendly give and take on the playground compares to the best of team building in the office. Playfulness makes it in the flow. Lightness of being brings inspiration. Play is tantamount to being in the *now* moment. The redeeming quality is that it allows one woman be herself to the maximum, with no thought of fear or failure. That is high play.

Trust, honesty, and go-with-the-flow spontaneity are the qualities of a leader at play. I play with words, and I especially enjoy playing with the alphabet. My alliterative lists of words are like high fun for me. I am making signs with these L words to remind me of my dedication to lightness of being. We found a welcome mat for the front door with "LIVE-LOVE-LAUGH" on it, and Janice, my daughter-in-law of nearly forty years now, gave me a yard sign with those same words. I have added other L words to complete my thoughts about playing all the time, even at work. They are new mottoes for me. What would they mean to you?

Words at Play

Live? What does it mean to you to be fully alive? To live to the maximum in a spirit of playfulness seems to be the best of the best life. Margaret Wheatley in her book *A Simpler Way* tells us that nature creates by "playfully mucking about." My experience tells me that play and creativity are closely connected. There is a presence, a newness, in play that is eternal. The now moment is our experience of eternity. So how long is now? And am I living in the now?

Love? I have come to know that love of self is my real test of whether I am playfully loving. I looked in the mirror this morning and sang the song from Fiddler on the Roof, "Do You Love Me?" The reflection in the mirror said, "I darn your socks—I floss your teeth," and I said again, "But do you love me?" and laughed out loud at the real dilemma. I probably have lived most of my life in a state of self-loathing rather than self-love. So how can I be playfully loving, especially to myself? Then I might lighten up and be more playful with my loved ones.

Laugh? My friend Amanda Jane Lukken (Amy) has learned to lead groups in laughter yoga. A cardiologist from India started this movement, and it is a wonderful stress reliever. I highly recommend laughing for no reason other than to laugh. It oxygenates your blood, it revives your brain, and it allows your body to return to equilibrium. Comedy is tragedy turned upside down. Norman Cousins wrote about healing himself with laughter.

I believe that laughter is one of our best ways to get relief. Relief is the beginning of healing.

Look? Open your eyes. What do you see? Pay attention to what happens next in your thoughts. Did you interpret what you saw? Is your interpretation more in the nature of a serious judgment? Can you be more playful in your interpretation? And then ask yourself, "What am I learning about myself?" Refresh your eyes by changing your judgmental thoughts and looking will bring joyful and playful experiences. We will change for the better when we can change our thinking instead of spending so much time on our appearance. Change your thoughts about how you look!

Listen? Can you listen in an attitude of playfulness? I watch little children playing, and they listen to parents and to each other. Then they usually return to play. When the parental words are serious and scolding, the play will usually incorporate that— scolding each other or scolding their dolls or animals. Listen to how children talk, and you will get a good idea of how playful the household conversation is.

Learn? The best learning is done when we are playful and light-hearted and have a good model to imitate. Children learn through imitation and play. Our learning can be meaningful when it has these elements. When learning is done in rote fashion, aimed at passing a test, it is no fun. Think back to your best learning and answer the question, "Was it fun?"

Liberate? You have talents, and you can liberate those talents. They can become your reliable strengths repertoire. You can liberate your thinking and your believing. If your beliefs are based in fear, then they will serve to keep you bound up in a sort of internal prison. If you are liberated, you can follow your curiosity and playfully examine any theory or any thought. We take ourselves and life so seriously. We deceive ourselves by believing that our serious certainty of mind is indicative of our maturity when it just may indicate our rigidity. Maybe we can

81

liberate our humor and live joyfully in a world that is playful. The real way to stay young is to be as playful as happy children.

Leave a legacy? I want my legacy to be remembered as one of joyful, happy, playful events and actions. Generosity and caring are best given without score-keeping. Altruism is like play in that it is done in the moment. It is charitable, and it is profoundly sincere.

I have spent a lot of time trying to think of a woman who illustrates the power of play and the advantage when a woman leader can lighten up. I thought of Ellen DeGeneres. She is a leader who is also a comedienne. She has the capacity to find humor and lightness of being in any human condition. I admire her authenticity and her presence in full life expression. She can dance in the best possible expression of her joy. There are others, of course. Maybe you can build your own list of women who know how to laugh.

Play Therapy

The person who brought play and the joy of lightening up to me is someone who champions women, has been my most effective developer, and happens to be male. I use him as a true example of the power of play. He is my partner in life and my best friend of the last forty-plus years: my husband, Paul.

Professor of education Dr. Marlyn Paul Barlow was retiring from Texas A&I University (now Texas A&M—Kingsville) in 1996. Our friend Dr. Garry Landreth was widely regarded as the dean of the whole world of play therapy for children. Garry recruited Paul to go back to school at the University of North Texas and become a registered play therapist. Paul did that and had a post-retirement career working with children, aged three to eleven, in his playroom. He had great success with children. Many of them got off the drugs they were given to keep them docile in their schoolrooms. It's no surprise that the majority of his clients were boys diagnosed with ADHD (attention deficit hyperactive disorder). Child-centered play therapy was the method Garry taught at the University of North Texas. After becoming a registered play therapist, Paul used Garry's ideas. He rigorously reflected the child's words and actions. He reflected feelings. Reflection was the heart of the method. There was no instruction, no admonishment, and no directives. These children had freedom of choice in how they played with the toys.

The playroom was restored to the same configuration after each session. The opening and closing was reliably the same for each time. The most amazing changes took place through the magic of forty minutes of play. Several of the boys seemed to need to test limits by throwing toys, splattering paint, or doing other "power" moves. They sometimes tied Paul up with the rope, handcuffed him, or other acts of taking control. After a few sessions of "trashing" the playroom, the most amazing change happened. There was a sort of settling into composure, and the outward behavior shifted from being highly destructive to playing in a more orderly and self-directed manner. Their locus of control shifted to being internally directed.

Example scenes included one young fellow making Paul a cup of tea in the play kitchen after six sessions of destroying the playroom. And he did this of his own free will, without ever being told to change, scolded for bad behavior, or asked to stop the destruction. His behavior wasn't changed for him; he chose to change it. He didn't change it to please the adult. He changed it because he felt safe in doing so and learned that it was the behavior most true to his inner self rather than the expectations of adults. His control shifted from outside to inside. He had been an obedient child, aiming to please and be perfect. He discovered that he could risk displeasure, make mistakes, and arrive at his own joyful self-direction. His natural, true self was the kind and caring young person who wanted to play at the art table and make a cup of tea for his friend Paul.

Play can transform us. Play can return our locus of control from outside to inside. Play releases us to let go of the shadow, engage fully in the moment, and creatively show up wherever we are. Work that feels like high play is in alignment with our calling.

Adults at Play

We experimented with adult play, using Paul's playroom for groups of adults who worked together. We were surprised at some of the reactions. One woman said, "I really don't know what it means to play." Another told us she remembered too many painful punishments associated with playing. One man painfully remembered being chosen last on every team. Each person had memories to talk about, and most of them said that they did not play much as adults. They reported that their lives were too busy to play. One owner of a company confessed that he takes vacations but usually ends up sick or injured. His life is normally work and no play.

There is no greater leadership than that of a leader who can bring a team or group into high play. Survival, thrival, belonging, self-esteem, and good feelings among the ones they lead are their legacy.

Fully engaged employees (who bring in and keep engaged customers) often tell me that their work is what they would do for fun. They rave about their job in glowing terms. They are fulfilled by their occupation, and they report favorably about their bosses and coworkers. These are the men and women who are working at something they are good at, where they are seen and recognized for their contribution, and where a spirit of play pervades the work environment. These are the people who have very few sick days, seem to spear-head high morale, and are great to be around. They are enlightened. They are engaged. Those who lead these teams are making the most from the human resources they are developing.

Alignment of mind with body coupled with expressions of emotion through play is healing to our stressful existence. Our bodies, according to quantum theory, are vibrational instruments. The heavy matter of our physical bodies vibrates at a certain frequency. Our emotional and mental "bodies" are vibratory also. We are energy in motion. When our energy is light and our mind, spirit, and body are aligned, we feel a lightness of being. Play is lightness of being in high form. Our mental and physical health will flourish in an atmosphere of play.

CHAPTER 6:

Wise Up

The Joy of Learning

Preparation: Facing the east, ponder your own growing wisdom. The star is Aldeberan in the zodiac constellation of Taurus. Taurus is an archetype for getting down to earth, and Aldeberan traditionally means the "one who sees." In some cultures, Aldeberan represents the mythical birth of new ideas. Think about yourself giving birth to the leader you can become. Dwell on your own unique and significant wisdom. The color is indigo blue. The goddess is Athena. Remember all the ways in which you have used your intellect to solve problems and create new possibilities. This meditation is about you as a wise and inventive leader.

The Wisdom of Servant Leadership

I had a really big experience this week. I have the great privilege of being a consultant to InterfaceFLOR. My work for them brought me to New York for a presentation on "How Full Is Your Bucket?" The InterfaceFLOR showroom is a beautiful facility with great design and all the stunning new products displayed. That in itself was a treat. The new carpet tiles are so beautiful and still are meeting the Zero Footprint goal of environmental sustainability. I am in awe of the responsible creativity from David Oakey and his design team.

But the real reason I am writing is to tell you about an organization that I learned about during the meetings. People have been losing jobs all across the country. This story is about a group that came together in New York to meet the crucial need of some of those people who are without employment temporarily. Architects and designers have been especially affected. Specifically, these were designers and architects willing to help each other in the downturn of this economic time. The majority of them were women.

LMNOP is the result of the innovative brainstorming of that small group. I met several of them on this trip and wish I could meet all of them, for they are the kind of people who face "what is" and meet the need, no matter what their own discouraging situation might be. That is the kind of pluck and courage that impresses everyone. Kristen Mucci and cofounder Stephanie Chiuminatto were there at the beginning of LMNOP, along with the other cofounder, Jennifer Graham. These women were at an event where they joined in the sharing of their loss of jobs. As a result of that conversation, they came up with this stunning idea: "Why not create an organization where we can help one another while we are looking for work?" After brainstorming for a while (wish I knew all the details of the birth of this project), they arrived at the brilliant idea—naming it LMNOP. The acronym stands for leadership, mentoring, networking opportunity for A&D professionals. You may know how much I love the alphabet, so this is the greatest idea ever to me!

They are talking now of making it a nonprofit organization, where people in the architecture and design industry can turn to one another for help. When you want to learn, when you need a mentor, when you want to spread the word about what you do, or when you want to search out new opportunities for jobs and services, LMNOP is there for you.

I grew up in the Great Depression, and LMNOP reminds me of the ways in which families, friends, and communities "made do" with what was, and we all got through it by being in it together. We *are* all in it together. If my neighbor is unemployed, if my friend has a need, or if my family calls, then I am called to respond. That's the way I want to be.

One other conversation on this trip was interesting for me. Someone asked if the strengths-based approach to life means that I can like everybody. I respect such a question, for it sort of suggests that my beliefs might be more like Polly Anna wearing rose-colored glasses and not facing up to the hard facts of reality. My reply was that I am a person who wants to like. In other words, I do not want my credo, my beliefs, or my manner of being to be determined by someone else's behavior. Whenever someone seems to be unlikeable, I go to that place of decision and choice. I ask myself, "How do I want to respond to this person?" My answer is that I want to be in the mode of liking, meaning I want to give the benefit of the doubt without judgment. I want to be coming from a loving heart, not a suspicious mind. And I have come to believe that when people are being unlikeable, it usually means that they are off track in their own purpose in life. Being likeable or lovable is not the same as having to compulsively please everyone. The neurotic drivers to be pleasing, be strong, or be perfect are conditions for false well-being. Surely I don't have to convince you that you won't please everyone, you are okay even if you are weak, and you can give up needing to be perfect. It is really okay to make mistakes. As Abraham-Hicks tells us, we weren't wrong or bad; we just weren't done yet. Every moment is a new beginning.

As a bonus, I discovered at the end of our meeting that Stephanie Chiuminatto, cofounder of LMNOP, is from Kingsville, Texas. I lived there for many years and knew Stephanie's grandparents and her parents! I can remember that little girl, Stephanie, who now has grown up and is pursuing her career in New York City. A small world! The connection was made in less than three degrees of freedom. We really are all in this together. All life is one. That is the deepest wisdom we can comprehend. We are *both* individuals *and* one life. Both/and is the stretch in thinking from the lonely place of separateness where everything is either/or.

The wisdom displayed by this group of young architects and designers, most of whom were women, was proof that we can have faith in the future. They do stand on our shoulders. Our shoulders are strong, broad, and capable of supporting future generations in their opportunities for evolutionary growth. They do evolve us, and we can therefore trust in the future. This is akin to faith, which is different from hope. Hope suggests that we are not sure, but faith says that we believe in the future. We are wise to do so.

Life-Long Learning

I am a learner. I learned this in my strengths assessment, obtained through the Clifton StrengthsFinder, which anyone can do by buying one of the books from the Gallup Organization. I took the assessment for the first time from the code in the back of the book by Donald O. Clifton and Marcus Buckingham, *Now, Discover Your Strengths.* Learner is one of my identified talents. My learning was stimulated in childhood. My mother was an elementary school teacher, and my father was a farmer and a bookkeeper. It was natural for them to teach me to read and do arithmetic. Mother also taught me to read music and play the piano, which was my entertainment in our home. We had no radio, TV, telephone, or computers—not even a manual typewriter. The piano was our greatest source of fun for me. Reading and doing arithmetic were fun too.

At age six, when I went to school, they promoted me to second grade since I already knew what they were to teach in the first grade. I devoured books. I read the cereal boxes, road signs, and anything that was in print. I graduated to funny books, Big Little

Books, and eventually to novels and philosophical books with deeper concepts. Today I have thousands of books and continue to buy shelves to hold more new books. I carry at least twenty books in my iPad so I can read anytime there is a break in the action. Does all this reading make me wise? No. Definitely no. Wisdom is different from the joy of learning. Wisdom is more a state of being that includes knowledge coupled with judgment, discernment, insight, and sagacity. Joy is pure delight, an emotion of happiness. Learning has to do with skills and mastery. So the joy of learning meant, for me, the sheer delight in discovery of ideas and concepts. Wisdom was born from deciding *what* to believe. This required intellectual honesty and trust in my own intuitive curiosity as to what I would learn. Skills and knowledge coupled with my basic talents form the basis for my strengths. My strengths path is the path of wisdom, joy, and learning. Over the years, I have met several mentors and teachers who provided for me the interest and intrigue to dive deeper into learning. One of those mentors was and is Jean Houston.

Dr. Jean Houston

I first met Dr. Jean Houston in Kingsville, Texas, in 1982. She came to conduct a program at our local Texas A&I University (which later became Texas A&M—Kingsville). The program was entitled "The Possible Human." That weekend started me on a new and expanded path of my own professional development, culminating in a book and a service to women. Those concepts became the Possible Woman, and I give Jean credit for being the muse who helped make it happen. On that day in 1982, I drove to the airport in Corpus Christi to give her a ride to Kingsville. She said I would know her by the book she carried, which was *Life Force*. I saw this imposing figure of a very impressive woman with long brown hair. She was holding her book, and I introduced myself. We began a relationship in that hour-long drive that has survived all these years. I still admire her strength, her vision, her compassion, and her genius. She is a true Athena woman with high intellect and rare courage. I consider Jean a world leader. She is the epitome of engagement, and she is a model of leadership in female form. She evokes wisdom from her students, and she embodies the evolutionary spiral of human wisdom. It is from Jean that I learned to question "Who am I?" and "What could I be?" These questions became my wisdom quest.

Women's wisdom is needed in leadership. What is different from the wisdom of men? Women are more cooperation-minded, and women naturally know how to collaborate. They are more horizontal than vertical in their thought process, more connected to the group, and more inclusive of everyone. Therefore, women who lead from their feminine mindset will be interested in diversity, in the wisdom of nature, and in the welfare of the entire community, family, or country—whatever she is leading. Women are closer to the earth, able to survive, and bear and nurture the babies of the human species, and most women embody true "systems thinking." Women intuitively and intrinsically know that we are all one life. We exist in connectedness to all life. We grow, we learn, we thrive, we withstand stress, and we are evolving survivors. Women are closer to the earth.

Future generations can include the ways of women and the wisdom of the female in the larger scene. There will come a time when corporations will have the unmistakable imprint of female leadership, creating a future for organizations serving the good of the whole of life in this universe. Women know how to nurture, to wait, to grow an idea, to listen, to bring a group together with the goal of forming a team, and to lead from that perspective. We are creating a future beyond the outmoded form where ideas are gathered, yet one person is really in control and leadership is a distortion of team building.

These ideas are not anti-male. They are evolutionary for the whole human race. I have watched men in leadership positions with some awe. My years as the breadwinner in my small family left me with great admiration for males who have been the sole support of their families for many generations. Many great men have brought great decision-making skills to their organizations. My curiosity drives me to ponder a world of parity where women share the privilege of leadership. I hope you will join me in wondering about the future in the light of possibilities. Women no longer need to bear thirteen babies and spend their entire life in the dependent roles of daughter, wife, and mother. I wonder what will happen when women are at true parity—in power and pay. I believe that the release of women to full partnership is also the means whereby men can be released to become fully human and fully alive. For the first time in human history, this partnership is possible. We live longer, we no longer need to have so many children, and with technology giving us its freedoms, we are able to create something new and very innovative in our world of work. The partnership way can explode our inventiveness in commerce as well as in child rearing.

Women represent the wisdom of nature. With the centuries of conceiving, gestating, birthing, and feeding the young, women have captured the wisdom born of survival—the life force that drives flowers to sprout and bloom. Women are "earthy"; therefore, they grasp the meaning of the botany and biology of life.

Males can sow the seeds and go away. They have done so over the millennia through necessity. Exploration, war, agriculture, ranching, technology, economics, and government have been the prime proving ground for the men of our societies. Women have stayed in the cave or the home, tending the young and old. It is the female of our species that held together the community, the family, and life at home when men went away to war or other exploratory adventures. Our future is a dream expanding beyond these past eons of power, control, strife, conquest, and dominance over each other.

These ideas are neither anti-male nor "imitation male." The release of women to full parity and participation is also an invitation to men to reach an expanded model of masculinity. It lessens the burden of giving one's total life over to making a living or foraging into new territory. Men in this twenty-first century can more fully participate in the necessary things of child rearing or tending the sick. Men and women can join together in our possibilities for space exploration and space colonization, which is becoming the "new west."

Generational Changes

Becoming a leader in these changing times requires that we understand the generations. When were you born? Where did you grow up? What were the cultural norms of your first twenty years? These questions will help you be aware of where you are in the evolution of culture during your lifetime. Awareness is the door to growth and understanding. Awareness precedes waking up. I invite you to explore your world.

To review the generational divide, think of your life and compare the statistical norms to your own individual patterns. If you, like me, were born before 1944, you have these qualities and characteristics that are born of your cultural programming: You like to have personal contact, eye to eye. You place your trust when the language is clear and to the point and you feel included. You have deep connections and feelings about money. You are fiercely loyal, and you will work without much recognition. You appreciate knowing how you can contribute. You may be digital dinosaurs, but you still want to be in communication, so you may need help from the younger generation.

If you were born in that period following World War II, you were the generation that called the world to task, insisted that we examine our values, and created the '60s revolution. You speak openly, frankly, and directly, and you appreciate being included in decisions. You might have tried communal living, and you adopted a strong work ethic. You embraced the song, "What the World Needs Now Is Love, Love, Love." You can communicate face to face or electronically, and you assume your uniqueness with ease. You are called Boomers, and you will carry forward your impact into post-retirement since there are so many of you.

If you were born between 1965 and 1980, we refer to you as Gen-Xers. In your career, you want freedom from the old style of management practices. You want room to be creative. You will be a multi-tracker, and you need opportunities to learn new skills. You may have several careers because you like variety. You are digital naturals and still may prefer to use email. Email and texting may have superseded face-to-face communication or the telephone. You appreciate flex-time, creativity, and multiple projects. Your leadership will respect work-life balance.

Millennials were born from 1980 to 2000. You want to know what is in it for you. You like media in multiple forms, and you have most of your focus on your own personal goals, but you will try to weave those into your job, which you want to be challenging and meaningful. You like feedback as long as it is a reciprocal dialogue, and you want to take on out-of-the-box challenges. You speak digital short-hand, are usually competitive and less formal, and you work to live—not the opposite, live to work. Your ideas about loyalty are different, and you may come across to older generations as having an attitude of entitlement. You want continuous feedback and expect everything to be at the push of a button.

Knowing your generation and understanding your motivational drivers will help as you bring out the leader who is inside you. One other way of looking at your leadership is to sub-divide your life into four categories of action. First, we have a personal life, which usually involves a significant other—spouse or spice. Second, we have a physical life in which we take care of the body we live in. Third, we have a career, which at best is also our calling. And fourth, we have beliefs in what might be called the supernatural or spiritual arena.

In the self-awareness that I advocate, you will do well to take time to look at yourself and measure the amount of energy you give to these four arenas. Then be aware of the generation in which you were born and assess how that has affected your beliefs, thoughts, feelings, and behaviors.

My parents were afraid of what my generation was learning and doing. They were of the Roaring Twenties era, and they feared that their children were going to "hell in a hand basket." That worry was evident when they expressed grave concern that Paul and I were buying a large house and it was to cost nearly fifty thousand dollars. Their thinking was still mired in the Great Depressions and all the sorrow they experienced over lack of money. I hear my friends talking about the coming generations with negative opinions. I suggest that each generation actually evolves the past generations. Our Veterans group has evolved the Roaring Twenties. The Baby Boomers are evolving the Veterans, the Gen-Xers are evolving the Baby Boomers, and the Millennials are evolving the Gen-Xers. Evolving means that they are creating something based on what has gone before, and like the Phoenix Bird rising from its own ashes. It then goes forth toward new and different structures that transcend the old ones. They stand on our shoulders, and they evolve us in the never-ending spiral of consciousness and growth.

Women's Wisdom Group

My generation evolved the previous generation. We do grow, and we do change. Each stage of life development brings learning, expansion, and growth in wisdom. We take what we learn and expand it. For years, I have had a women's wisdom group. We meet to report our lives to each other, to give support and encouragement, and to laugh and eat together. Out of these social meetings have come changes in thinking, habits, and other life-saving or enhancing inspirational wisdom. No longer is it a group where everyone brings complaints, criticism, or castigations. We have long ago given up that as a means of change. Instead, the individual women in the group are into creativity. They really have moved beyond whining and complaining. They bring their newest ideas and creations. They solve problems in ways that do not limit their loved ones to judgment. And most important, we laugh a lot. Life is joyous for this sisterhood.

These incredible women are diverse and individual to the maximum. One of them has great taste in décor, color, and style and sometimes brings her sketches. Another brings her human development expertise, sharing her latest innovations in teaching and guiding young people. Another shows up with books that explain her teenage child's behavior. One of these wise women amazed us with her marriage and subsequent move to another state. Another reports on her latest art show where she exhibited her creative pottery and paintings. We discovered that one of these women is an expert on the economic scene, and she shares her insights on investing. Her son is a new model male, studying to be a nurse practitioner.

In our meetings, we may talk about gardening or having fun on the job while expanding spiritual practices. Some of them have created active and successful businesses. At least three in our group are professional musicians, performing and teaching all ages. Others get real about serious physical illnesses. We talk philosophically about death and dying. One has created an ingenious method with her "Omega papers," helping us prepare for our last party, our funeral. Transition is often the topic as we move from career into retirement. Women's peculiar body realities—from broken bones to menopause—are shared with great empathy and information. We exhibit pathos and optimism at every meeting. We valiantly create the next life, building from the ashes of the past. We create loving friendships, we face our co-dependencies, we talk with hope and humor, and we never give up.

This group is open and continually changing. There is never a meeting that is the same as before. Our wisdom group is like the Nueces or Guadalupe Rivers, in that the name creates an identity, but the river is ever shifting and changing so that it is never ever predictable or "settled." And so it is with our group. We continue to be present for each other in our circle meetings. We are open and accepting, loving and caring, and of course, very *wise*. Perhaps the greatest wisdom of all in this wisdom group is that we laugh a lot and seem to always find life to be entertainingly funny. In many of our meetings, we have laughed until our sides hurt. Sometimes we cry too. This group of women is very genuine and very real. To me, our women's wisdom group is the epitome of the Possible Woman stepping up.

The friendship and closeness of these women is suggestive of Dr. Jean Bolen's *Millionth Circle*. In that book, Jean proposes that when the millionth women's circle meets, we will have a change in the world. Such groups form informally and by design. Women tend to bond and join each other in like-minded groups. We are more horizontal in our management and less pyramidal or vertical in our thinking.

The Shape of Things to Come: From Pyramid to Circle

Our world is changing. We are no longer living with our triangular structures of the past. In the old pyramidal or triangular structures, there was a boss, a teacher, a parent, or a manager who sat at the top of the pyramid. The orders came from above, and obedient people carried them out. Even the United States Army is now teaching that every troop is an army of one. In our wisdom circles, we believe that there is a leader in every chair. The first person you lead is yourself. Your own wisdom is tapped with every choice you make. Just as a lone soldier must make decisions in an instant, so can we. In fact, women have been doing that type of management for centuries. We come by this style very naturally because of the natural configuration of our bodies. We are, by our very nature, designed to collaborate, to create, and to change. We have a connection at the deepest levels.

At the Vancouver Peace Summit in 2010, the Dalai Lama said something that ricocheted around the world in an instant. He said that he is a feminist. He offered his opinion that Western women will save the world. At that same conference, Abigail Disney presented her film, *Pray the Devil Back to Hell*. It tells the story of a group of Liberian women ousting a dictator and installing their first female president. Many other powerful women were present at that conference, paying witness to the rise of women's leadership. Western women have economic, sexual, and reproductive freedom. When all the women on Earth have that, we will have a different existence and a better life on this planet. Women have values that will promote life and prevent us from destroying our civilization. The freedom enjoyed by Western women is a dream for the future of all women.

Women study, women learn, and women are familiar with the driving force of emotions. Most of the people in my therapy practice were women. Much of our work in the Possible Woman seminars is involved with uncovering our pain, the dark side of emotion, and getting to know our shadow. C. G. Jung gave us the concepts of the collective unconscious and the shadow. Simplified, I think he normalized the angel and the devil in each of us. And he revealed that at some level, we are all connected. Our wisdom is a pool of evolutionary wisdom, built over thousands of generations of human beings. Our shadow, the dark side, has also been developed over eons of our history. It is the contrast that shows us where wisdom can aid in our evolution. Humans are a species moving in the wheel of time through our various evolutionary identities. We were nomadic wanderers, we were agrarian age farmers, we have been technological geniuses, and now we embark on the age of ideas, the Aquarian age. We are capable of and we are learning to recognize our ideas, question them, and stop believing the ones that are detrimental to our expansive evolutionary growth. We are learning that awareness is the door opening to our wisdom. We are connected, we can be aware, and we can learn. We can be wise.

There is a beautiful film called, *It's in Every One of Us.* The music, written by David Pomeranz, says, *"It's in every one of us:*

To be wise
Find your heart
Open up both your eyes,
We can all know everything
Without ever knowing why.

It's in every one of us ... to be wise ... open up both your eyes."
The fading images morph into the next face, and we see that we are one. We can be wise.

CHAPTER 7:

Link Up

The Joys of Relationship

Preparation: While facing north, meditate on your relationships. Ponder what vibrational energy means. Sense the ultimate vibration of love. The star is Vega, the Master of Sound. In your imagination, follow a light beam to Vega, and return full of your own music. The color is violet. The guiding mythological figure is the goddess Hestia, guardian of hearth and home. Meditate or think about music, dance, and joyful celebrations that include your closest relationships. Feel the warmth of love radiating from your heart center. Experience the security of home. Bask in the feelings of unconditional love.

We Are All in This Together

The year was 2003, and I was dealing with my mother's end-of-life issues. She was a loving person who made it easy for my brother and me. She moved to our city and lived out her last months in a warm, caring, loving community. Our lives were enriched, and we shared many memorable times with her. I felt alive and happy in her presence, and her gift was the treasure of her ability to love unconditionally. Linking up with a beloved family member taught me more about relationships. Altogether, I was realizing that we are all linked to each other.

Our relationships are the tumbling vat in which we come up against each other like raw stones. We bump up against each other. We are shined, cracked, and stretched. The simple truth of relationships that I have embraced is that we grow into our best selves when we learn to take the path of love. Love is the warm acceptance of another human being (and ourselves) just as he or she is. Our relationships are the grist for the mill of our refinement. Parents and other family members are the most intimate and carry the most possibilities for growth. Friends and other acquaintances make up the next circle of relationship potential for growth.

My work as a consultant has been primarily focused on relationship repair, restoration, evolution, and change. My certainty that the positive approach is best gave me the courage to see any relationship as a potential path of growth. Whenever a rift happens, we have two choices. We can either go into fear, attempting to control, comply, or quit, or we can recognize the invitation to learn how to love. The same belief applies to business relationships. The people with whom we work offer the probability that we will re-create our family of origin, and all the unfinished emotional business will show up at work, still needing to be faced and resolved. My favorite story involved two highly talented young men who could not get along with each other. I was asked to work with them and did so in the presence of their team members. The breakthrough came when each recognized old, unfinished family patterns showing up in their current relationship. They were open to learning about the defense mechanism called projection. Projection is where we see in others those things that are still in the abscess of our shadow or our unconscious mind. These things show up in real life to provoke us to grow past the wounds of childhood. One man was the first born in a large family; the other was last born in his large family. The obvious sibling rivalry and leftover bad feelings were showing up again in their current world of work. We worked with their homesickness and held difficult conversations in which they could find new solutions without returning to the old limiting roles of big and little brothers.

Grandmother in Residence

In the same time frame that my mother moved into our city for the final six months of her life, I was working for a corporation as a relationship coach. I was hosting several regional vice presidents from that company. They would come in for a day or two just to get away and think about the future. This program has morphed into what I now call, "Grandmother in Residence." It simply means that I offer a retreat for busy executives to get away from daily responsibilities. They come, and we look at their life story from birth to death. We construct genograms (emotional family trees), we do time lines, and we do other exploratory venturing into the depths of their beliefs, thoughts, feelings, and behavior. Or we do little more than talk with each other, depending on how far they want to go into the deep awareness of individual development. The gratification comes with the luxury of a no-pressure time, a candid look at relationships, and almost without exception, the realization that they are an integral part of the oneness of all life.

My observation is that we are more productive and the meetings are more fruitful because we are not doing therapy but are discovering possibilities for growth. My intention is that it be about their unfolding, not their molding. The subject is the deep awakeness and lucid living that come when a person is self-aware and self-accepting. If self-forgiveness is needed, we go there too. If current problems need to be solved, we brainstorm all the possibilities. We glean the depths of their talents, and we uncover the essence of their authentic godseed. We discuss being separate and being part of the whole. The polarity of individual self-development, coupled with the opposite pole of integration into all of life, makes for lively conversation. I am always pleased when their eyes light up, as if something has dawned and something new is ready to come forth. Most report that they are satisfied with what this private retreat gives them—they got what they came for. One executive said it was sort of like drinking from a fire-hose. He is still in his turning point of leaving one company and resolving his future. Without exception, each one sees the link to their relationships as being the key component in triggering what still needs to grow. Relationship with self is first (and that includes relationship with what they call the divine); relationship with family and friends is next. The central common denominator is the person whose life is being examined. This person joining the triple A and becoming author, actor, and audience in his or her life story is also part of the outcome.

These meetings are so real, the people are so genuine, and the optimism that floats to the surface with their discoveries about the mechanics of good relating to others is exciting and full of possibilities. One of the best concepts that we use is that of twisting the Golden Rule. Tom Rath and Don Clifton made this one of their strategies in *How Full Is Your Bucket?* Imagine that you can change the golden rule from doing unto others as we would have them do to us to the more relationship-oriented version: "Do unto others as they would like to be done unto." This means we must get to know one another, making friends, and understanding each other's needs, wants, and feelings. Understanding is the key component that I watch as people make their change from being an individual who judges, blames, whines, and complains to an individual who is really interested in other people and their development. There has been an amazing response, and I will continue offering these "Visits to Grandmother's house" as long as there is a demand. Paul helps with every detail of these retreats, so it really should be re-titled, "A Visit to the Grandparents." We have enjoyed sharing our new, down-sized home with these friends.

I uncovered a revelation in my life at the same period of time when I was creating the private positive retreats for business partners and moving on past my loss of my mother. Everything anyone was experiencing in the stories brought to the Grandmother Retreat was also a part of my own personal journey. I share with you my own human fallibility. As they discussed their resentments and frustrations, I was reminded of my own. Even though I know and I have taught that believing our thoughts is the root of our suffering, I still am prone to revert to type and fall off in the ruts of complain, whine, judge, and criticize. The following is a personal confession to let you know that I am human and I learn from my trips into fear also.

From My Personal Journal
October 14, 2004

> What is it about making the oatmeal? If he chooses to put in half a cup instead of one full cup, why is that important to me? I felt my resistance and my insistence rising today when I saw that he had measured out only half the required amount of oatmeal and therefore was making only one serving. The table was set for two, so I would be getting half my normal serving. Was that what it was about? Not getting enough? No. It was more about not getting my way. After all, I have perfected the cooking of five-minute oats. You put in two cups of water, add six prunes cut into six pieces each (using the black-handled kitchen scissors), and then you add half a teaspoon of salt and two packets of Splenda sweetener. And there he was, with only one cup of water, one-half cup of oats, and he was cutting the prunes crudely with a knife. I rose to defend my battle station. I confronted his method, his action, and his character. Well, I was sort of

nice about it. I asked (just like his mother used to ask), "Are you just cooking half a cup of oats?" That, to him, meant he made a mistake (old program from childhood), and on and on the drama unfolded.

He finally resorted to using his play therapy technique, asking me, "Is this the way you want it?" That meant he had caught on first that we were in a mortal battle for survival, and we were in the toddler stage (or maybe three- or four-year-olds) of development. "This is mine" "I am right" versus "No, this is mine!" "You are wrong," and the power struggle was engaged ...

All that training, all that study of the unconscious mind, all that growing up, and I am still not really grown up. How embarrassing. I thought I was beyond the pain of needing to have my way. But I am not. No sirree, I am not.

Just don't you forget, I know how to cook oatmeal! My way is the *right way!* I would rather be right than happy. That is what makes me a righteous person. So there! As Poppie Mac used to say, "Nuph sed."

He also said often, "On we go!" so I said, "Can we just have breakfast and get on with it!"

Afterward, I retreated to my own safe place and meditated on what had happened. Self-forgiveness was difficult but necessary. Refreshed eyes, accurate ears, and a nonjudgmental attitude helped me laugh at my own retreat into childhood patterns. There seems to be wisdom in taking myself less seriously, especially as it always affects my closest relationships. My newest, deep discovery is that the past is over and can no longer hurt us. I quoted Byron Katie to one of my children recently. Katie said to her daughter, who was complaining about Katie's mothering: "I was a perfect mother. I was responsible for all your problems. You are responsible for their solutions!"

In that same vein I can say to Paul, "I was a perfect wife. I was responsible for provoking all your problems. You are responsible for their solutions."

Life lesson learned from this journaling: My contribution to the relationship can be negative or positive. When my ego is threatened, I tend to revert to fear and try to get control, or I suck it in and hold the anger and resentment in my thoughts. The only power I hold is the power of recognition of my projections and the realization that I cannot ever control another human being without his or her cooperation. The best relationships get to this state of non-codependence. Being together and maintaining our autonomy is the greatest gift we receive from doing the stretching required by close relationships. Relationships allow us to learn how to love. From scenes like this one, I now say, "It is easy to love them when they act right. No stretch there!"

Leading *Is* Relating

Relationships are what most leadership is all about. Relationships are what sales are all about. Relationships are what life is all about. It is easy to go away and be alone if you want to think, to ponder, to relax, and to not be bothered. There is no conflict or contrast in solitude. Linking up with another human being, being in a group, becoming a member of a team, and working with any collection of individuals is the real challenge to life on the planet. You could go off to a mountain retreat and live in quiet, meditative solitude for as long as you could tolerate your own self. But eventually you will probably need or want to come back into the mix of the crowd, the city, the family, or the corporation. And then your learning will continue—your stretching is inevitable.

So how do we link up in relationships and still remain the

individual we were meant to be? This chapter is about that all-important facet of human existence—living in relationship with others. I made a living off of this phenomenon. Relationships were my area of study and still are. I started with my childhood and the relationship with my mother, father, grandfather, and aunt—my family of origin. Those relationships were the mold and the model for my approach to all relationships. The very nature of being born small and dependent is that we start life as victims. We are codependent from the beginning since our very small bodies are vulnerable, and we need protection from our caretakers. The way that protection and well-meaning action, their parenting, was done has shaped our brains and minds to the point that we project outwardly and onto others what we came to expect as little people under the age of eleven. The way our parents talked to us and the way they ministered to our needs for security, food, and cleanliness shaped the way we meet and react to others today. Children learn from imitation and play. We imitate our parents and other caretakers—their language, their behavior, and even their emotional patterns.

Waking up from the trance of childhood is part of growing up. Owning our projections is part of waking up. Projection is a defense mechanism that helps us cope. We need it, and we use it until we don't need it any more. Basically we have a projector that runs inside us. When we are still in the trancelike state, we don't really know that we attribute to others the very qualities, good or bad, that we hold within ourselves. We unconsciously project the heads of our family-of-origin members onto the shoulders of our coworkers and intimate relationships. We continue to do that until we begin to come out of the trance. Our subconscious mind harbors all these defenses, and they are helpful in our survival. The more we can bring our subconscious mind into consciousness, the more we spiral in our own path toward authenticity. Our awakening is ever calling us to more consciousness. We wake up through the process of what I call "merciless self-awareness." The rule of thumb is that if you are experiencing a negative emotion, you may be projecting something from inside yourself, something from your own subconscious mind. You don't know about it consciously.

Let me explain. When Paul and I get into an argument, you can be sure I am at some level of my consciousness projecting my father onto him. He, in turn, projects his mother onto me, and that is what our work as a couple has been in order for us to mature into more of a grown-up kind of love. My father was very controlling and Paul's mother was also a controller, so perhaps you can imagine what happens in our arguments. Each of us thinks the other is trying to control. Paul tends to rebel, just as he did with his mother. I tend to obey but sulk, just as I did with my father. Now you would think two eighty-year-olds would know better, but we still get trapped in these old patterns. We test our level of consciousness every day, and I am happy to say, most days we realize when we are still in the automatic, robotic reactions learned in our childhood. We just say that we must have been homesick. Then we laugh at ourselves and get back to the business of being adults in a successful relationship.

One very successful and productive corporate executive took issue with the notion of projection. He said, "I cannot see how I am projecting in this situation." The situation was that his employee was habitually whining and complaining, believing that she was being mistreated. The executive said that he had given her many privileges, and she was never grateful. Basically he went on to complain that she was mistreating him. I reflected his words as he spoke about her. At the end of the conversation, he had an aha moment where he saw his own complaining and whining and his belief that he was being mistreated. This scene is played out almost every day in relationships at work.

I have had many instances where one person seemed to be at an impasse with another, and when we got to the root of the situation, each had gone home again. I think of therapy as synonymous with growth, and my encouragement to everyone is to keep growing. Stay in some form of self-awareness therapy or self-study. Lucid living is like lucid dreaming, where you actively participate in the scenario, allowing that you are composing it, directing it, and acting in every scene of the drama of your life. The need for such growth is always indicated when there is dissension in relationships. The signal that work is needed is the negative emotion, the bucket-dipping, the criticism, caustic remarks, sulking, gossip, or other faultfinding that is going on. Like toxic pollution in environmental circumstances, negativity toward others in our relationships is damaging to the social environment.

I will offer you my saying, Scripture-like, on projection: "Whatsoever thing thy neighbor doeth that rattleth thy cage, ringeth thy bell, puncheth thy button, or pulleth thy chain, that thing hath more to do with thee than with thy neighbor! But take heart, thy neighbor is thy friend, offering thee the path to thine own growth. Own thine own projection and thou shalt be carried on the river of fulfillment of thine own destiny—becoming thine own true self."

Linking up with other human beings may be the prime purpose for our living here on this planet. In conjunction with our fellow human beings, we can do great things. When we are in divisive, warring relationships, we do a lot of damage. Wars are often the solution when relationships break down. Divorce, murder, suicide, or other forms of drastic solutions are often the choices we make. The interesting and depressing fact is that war, punishment, divorce, murder, suicide, and other forms of trying to solve relationship problems do not work. Our prison system is an indicator that punishment does not rehabilitate people into becoming productive citizens. The recidivism rate is proof of that. Punishment does not improve relationships. Moreover, changing jobs, changing partners, and changing outside circumstances will not bring a better life. As my cousin said after five marriages and four divorces, "In every relationship, I took myself along. I was the common denominator, and I had to get real about me. What I expected in the relationship was invariably what I got."

A developmental approach is needed. All relationships are like babies that need to be tended. They are like bank accounts, which need deposits as well as withdrawals. Loving relationships are the hope of the human race. We can learn to live together, we can learn to love one another, and we can grow up as human beings. The future model of us human beings will be expanded to use our heart brain as well as our head brain.

If you are seeking help for an intimate, committed relationship, I recommend that you invest in a weekend of Imago Relationship Education.[2] Imago Relationship Therapy was one of the best I ever used in my career as a marriage and family therapist. There are excellent books and many good therapies for couples. Even though it takes great courage to risk such growth, it is worth doing, and I encourage you to try. All relationships, personal and professional, teach us about ourselves. And all relationships are the laboratory in which we learn about love.

Love comes in different flavors, different expressions, and different behaviors.

The Ladder of Love

There is a four-rung ladder of love, with the first rung being eros or sexual love. That is the attraction in intimate relationships, and it is the kind of love that keeps our species alive. Without eros, we would not be attracted to each other, and the race would probably die out. The second rung of this ladder is called "agape" love. This is the love that says we can live together in harmony and peace. Agape love means that I have respect for our relationship and will engage in acts of caring toward you. It is the way of diplomacy, mediation, peacekeeping, and mutual friendship. The third rung

---

2   For more information on Imago Relationships, visit
     gettingtheloveyouwant.com.

of the ladder is philea or brotherly love. When I experience brotherly love, I see you as part of my family; you are one of my clan. Philadelphia, Pennsylvania, is known as the city of brotherly love, using the root word philea. The fourth rung of the ladder of love is caritas, which means charity. Charity is that sacrificial love that says, "I will turn the other cheek and give you the coat off my back when you ask for my shirt." Charity is Christ love.

When we relate to another person, there is a pathway toward something that represents our connectedness, our sacred link in the truest and best sense of the word. That pathway will lead to one of the four kinds of love. Whenever a relationship has reached some sort of discord, we have departed from the path. Usually that departure is toward some sort of relationship destruction— the path of fear. There are three responses to the fear path—to control, to comply, or to quit. In other words, when I am at the place in a relationship where I feel sure that I must get control of this person or be controlled by them or else we must sever our relationship, then I can know that I have quit learning to love and that I am following the path of fear.

People in healthy relationships may argue, yell, rage, and share very negative feelings. The reason that a relationship can do those things and still be healthy is in the concept of ownership. Each individual in relationship owns his or her own beliefs, thoughts, feelings, and behavior. That means that I can be mad and still stay in relationship because I will not blame or otherwise attribute ownership of my anger to you. I will tell you I am mad and that your behavior has triggered it, but I will not make you responsible for my anger. Our conversation can be about what triggered my anger and the consequences to me of that anger. You can put your emotional armor on and listen to my anger without taking responsibility for it. You can admit the behavior, and yet you have no wires or buttons to my emotions. Therefore, you have no power to own my anger or to even cause it. The old "make-feel" theory is hard to forget. As children, we were told such things as, "You

111

made your brother cry," "You are giving me gray hair," "You will be the death of me," or other dire consequences. We grew up in a world where we really believed that we made someone mad, sad, or glad. In turn, we believed that they made us feel what we felt. These are false, codependent beliefs, rooted in attachment theory. They hold us in the superstitions of the past. We can, and we are required for evolutionary purposes, get beyond those old false beliefs.

Your relationships at your work or in your career are a key to your own growth. Based on my experience serving the corporate world for many years, I suggest that you first learn how to hold difficult conversations. Listening for content, validation for meaning, and empathy for feelings are invaluable skills when relationships on the job are in trouble. You will do well to recognize the need for more positive than negative dialogue. John Gottman's longitudinal study of engaged couples revealed the startling but true statistic that any long-lasting relationships have a five to one ratio of positive to negative statements. The same ratio applies in the business setting with employer-employee relationships. One negative interaction will be neutralized if five positive interactions follow.

All positive change starts with examination of beliefs. Our relationships thrive when we can accept the other as a person of worth. Both personal and professional relationships require our stretching into vital friendship mode. Believing that we can become friends is the starting point. When we can interact without judgment, blame, criticism, or faultfinding, we will be more adult and mature in our relationships. Friends are adept at acceptance without conditions. And unconditional acceptance is actually possible when we grasp the nature of being the individual that we are—separate yet in connection. Linking up is easier when we really can be clear where we end and the other begins. Setting clear boundaries, being responsible for our own experience, and willingness to explore and learn about each other are the hallmarks of good relationships. Friendship is the best of all relationships, even in marriage.

Observation of great relationships over the years has revealed certain characteristics: 1) recognition that learning and growth are ongoing—each is a work in progress; 2) acceptance that spiritual, mental, and emotional belief systems are held up to the light of perceived truth and ever-changing—respect for individuality; 3) expansion of concepts and beliefs—appreciation for curiosity. The ancient teachings from many cultures plus current theories of relationships include learning about yin and yang, family scripts, communication practices, shadow work, the collective unconscious, brain development, child development, geriatrics, theology, and anything that is written about human relationships. Great relationships seem to foster a thirst for knowledge about how human beings relate to one another. Great relationships promote deep friendship. Family relationships provide a laboratory for learning about relationships. Professional work relationships furnish opportunities to learn about self, others, and the society or culture we live in. The ultimate best satisfaction comes from relationships that follow an intention to become friends.

Friends

> *Oh, the comfort—the inexpressible comfort of feeling safe*
> *with a person—having neither to weigh thoughts nor*
> *measure words, but pouring them all right out, just as they*
> *are, chaff and grain together; certain that a faithful hand*
> *will take and sift them, keep what is worth keeping, and*
> *then with the breath of kindness blow the rest away.*
> —Dinah Craik (written in 1859)

Friends promote and experience harmony, accord, understanding, and rapport. We feel affection and personal regard for our friends. We support our friends and work to stay on good terms with them. Friends are our chums, our comrades, our cronys, our confidantes,

113

our compatriots. Allies, and advocates. They have our back and we return the favor.

What do friends do when disaster strikes? On September 4, 2005, Hurricane Katrina devastated the city of New Orleans and other cities in Louisiana. Our thoughts of empathy, horror, and sympathy were followed with questions of how we could help. We were linked, emotionally and spiritually, to these survivors of Katrina. They were our friends. Eventually many of them arrived in our city of Corpus Christi, seeking refuge and looking for relief. What could we do to provide relief? First, they needed survival conditions, so our city provided shelter in the coliseum for five hundred people. Second, they needed to be safe and know that their homes in New Orleans were safe, so our city provided communication and other services in the nature of safety. Next, following Maslow's hierarchy needs, they needed to know they still belonged and could rely on the people around them. Many of these five hundred stayed in Corpus Christi because their homes were destroyed in New Orleans, and they found a new life in this new city where they were assured they could belong. Self-esteem followed when they obtained jobs and resumed their daily lives. They moved out of the coliseum and either returned to New Orleans or found new homes in new places. Good friendships, good relationships, and good neighbors are all part of linking up and realizing that we are all in this together.

I am writing today in 2011, and a crushing earthquake has just hit the nation of Japan. Our world is subject to enormous destruction. I am watching the pictures of the effects of the tsunami that followed the earthquake, which registered 9.0 on the Richter scale, the largest ever recorded in Japan. The threat of radiation from the nuclear power plant is adding more horrible drama to the story. We know that we are linked up since our communication now is instant and fast. We witness the rescue efforts from the comfort of our own living room. There is an outpouring of empathy from friends across the globe.

The link-up of our entire planet is like a neuronal network in the brain of Gaia, our living planet home. Facebook, Twitter, and all the innovative gifts of the Internet have connected us. I said years ago that communism fell because of fax machines; they could not keep the secret of the rest of the world hidden any longer. That tongue-in-cheek analogy is even more applicable today. We are experiencing a massive upheaval brought about by social networking. Egypt and Libya are experiencing the backlash from oppression. The stories suggest that the uprisings are made possible through the social media, the linking up of individuals, which can forge together a movement that changes a nation.

We may be at the end of times. Without doubt, the past is over. Living in the now moment spells the end of time as we know it. Our relationships are the means through which we experience space-time. Joining with one another in peaceful, friendly relationships will herald a new age. Peace and harmony can be the result of all the threats to existence, whether they are natural phenomena like earthquakes or hurricanes or human upheavals like rebellion and uprisings. We might just learn how to love one another and live as good friends on this fair planet, our island home. Then we will be at the beginning of times—a new time—a new age.

In *Vital Friends* by Tom Rath, I learned about eight categories of friends. Rath's research revealed that we have friends who might be builders, champions, companions, mind openers, energizers, navigators, collaborators, or connectors. These are our links to one another. One friend will be a builder, someone who takes an interest in us as we grow. Another will be our champion, bringing us to our higher development through their belief in us. My husband, Paul, is my companion friend. He has also been my mind opener friend in our long marriage. I have several lovely friends who are connectors, introducing me to new people and making sure I am included. Other friends are navigators to whom

I can go when I need to be shown the way or need good advice. And all of us need energizer friends who will bring fun into our lives. These categories of friendships are a great description of the categories of good relationships.

Essentials of a Good Relationship

In summary, these are needed if any relationship is to be satisfying, fulfilling, and growth-provoking:

1. Awareness, especially self-awareness, which is the door to growth and change. Your relationships will improve when you are fully aware and have full responsibility for your assumptions, your interpretations, your judgments, your competition for innocence, and your belief that everything is about you.

2. Practicing the principle of being both observer and participant in all interactions. This essential can be roughly translated as the need to let go of your need to be right.

3. Risking authenticity, "courageous realness," and genuineness. The real risk is that you will be known, you will be seen, you will be transparent, and you will be changed. Trust your intuition and obey your instincts, listening to that wee, small voice that is your authentic soul-self.

4. Responsible ownership, which is the maturity principle. It means that a good relationship needs each person to be grown up. A business executive recently told me that his meetings are productive because each person leaves his or her ego at the door when the meeting starts.

5. All relationships mature and get better when each person takes personal responsibility for beliefs, thoughts, feelings, and behavior. It really is all an

inside job. You can accept the internal flow of meaning that you attribute to the other one. You can know that your own perception creates your reality and that your projections create your perceptions. You have the power to choose your responses. Growing up means that you no longer blame the other. You can decide whether the universe is friendly or hostile. You can learn the true meaning of love.

6. Wise choices, which means deciding to be creative rather than reactive. You can know when you are off track in your own development. Confusion, resistance, resentment, or any negative emotion is the signal that change is necessary. You are able to change when you examine your thoughts, question your beliefs, and realize that you are creating the experience. You can be impeccable in your word. You can listen to yourself and live according to your own values. You can know yourself and even understand your brain, your beliefs, your thoughts, and your assumptions. You can learn new concepts, and together with the other person, you can establish a positive relationship vision.

7. Mindful communication. You can create new ways of thinking together. You can observe the conversation as more than talk, actually understanding that the conversation *is* the relationship. You can create through the power of your own intention a pathway to love rather than traveling the road of fear. Fear leads to the need for control, compliance, or withdrawal, and you can decide to stay in the relationship. You can be aware of your words, your voice tone, your facial expression, and your body postures, gestures, and movements. You can choose to be the person you want to be even in the stress and strain of a testy relationship. Growing up means learning new skills

and gaining new knowledge about the value of relating. Ongoing skill building. You can hear accurately, without blame, judgment, or criticism. You can see the other person through fresh, new, soft eyes. You can be the support person for another, holding the field of possibilities while he or she finds his or her way. You can invest in the development of the other, trusting that he or she will rise to his or her possibilities. You can spend time being a flat mirror, practicing reflection (the words), validation (the meaning), and empathy (the feelings). You can learn how to hold difficult conversations resulting in better decisions.

8. Comfortable silence. You can let silence do the heavy lifting. Silence is golden; silence is wisdom. You can grow into a real connection by being there, being sensitive, and being quiet.

We link up with our coworkers. We link up with our customers. We link up with each other in groups, teams, meetings, gatherings, games, and many other activities that are communal and bring us together. Those links form a strong chain of relationships, connecting us to each other with the hope of positive possibilities. Playing in a band, joining a knitting group, and meeting with others who have our same interests are all ways of linking up. Someday the whole tribe of the planet might link up, and on that day, we will have discovered the power of love, which will be the greatest thing since we discovered fire. The possible human will be evolved into a new model. We will thrive, not just survive, we will follow our emotional guidance, we will know how to think creatively, and we will be altruistically able to love one another. We will have stepped up into a new age.

CHAPTER 8:

Offer Up

The Joy of Work

Preparation: Look to the south, and imagine that you can visit the distant star Syrius, known as the Dog Star. Some cultures say Syrius is the Way Shower. Your mission is the way that shows up in your career. Spend a few minutes thinking about the vision of yourself as a leader who knows how to show the way. Stay open to outcomes, letting your fertile imagination guide you. The color is magenta, representing your highest and best version of yourself. The archetype is your high self—your authentic being—the you of you that you were destined to become. Dream your most expansive dream of yourself and your contribution to the universe of your personal life, your career, and your journey. Name the deep truth, the values, and the possibilities that reveal your maximum self-development. Meditate on your legacy. What are you contributing to the good of your world through your work?

Post-Retirement Work

The year was 1994, and I was nearing the traditional retirement age of sixty-five. I wrote in my journal many times that year about what I would do in retirement. The result was a "dream job" that I concocted where I would be able to continue what I loved to do most—listen to people and stand with them while they found their own pathway to a more desirable life. I wanted to continue soliciting members of the AAA, which was my hypothetical organization that people could join, becoming author, actor, and audience in their own life story. I wanted this post-retirement job to include travel, telephone appointments, and weekend workshops or seminars. I also wanted to continue my post-doctoral studies in many subjects. I wanted to get more familiar with environmental sustainability, with group dynamics, positive psychology, and my usual dabbling in theology and other esoteric subjects, such as astrology.

The next year brought an invitation to do some hourly work at InterfaceFLOR (then called Interface, Inc.), the global modular carpet manufacturing company. Now, fifteen years later, I am realizing that my dream job is reality. I work as a consultant, strengths coach, and relationship coach for InterfaceFLOR. My daily job includes appointments by telephone, Skype, iChat, or conference calls. I travel. I get to make speeches. I do seminars and weekend workshops, cruises, and spa retreats for women. I continue to advance my penchant for learning through training with the teachers I like best. My life is a model for women. If I can do it, you can do it. The only caveat is the job *must* be something you enjoy and have a talent for doing.

Sustainability

We are serving the needs of the future generations—tomorrow's children. We can use sustainable methods. Environmental sustainability is a crucial task, and women can lead in that task. As

Ray C. Anderson, founder of InterfaceFLOR and environmental crusader, said, "The ascendency of women in business is coming just in the nick of time. It is that instinctive nurturing nature, found more frequently in women, but also present in men if they will allow it to surface, that will recognize and elevate in business the vital, indispensable role of genuine caring. Caring for human capital and natural capital (Earth) as much as we traditionally have cared for financial capital will give social equity and environmental stewardship their rightful places alongside economic, progress, and move society to reinvent the means for achieving economic progress itself." *Mid-Course Correction, Atlanta, GA, Peregrinzilla Press, 1998.pp 185-186.*

Sustainability is a natural avenue for women's leadership. Economic, environmental, and social sustainability are ready-made for women's strengths. When third-world countries receive financial aid, that money is often subverted from its intended mission. Funds sometimes go toward corruption and the purchase of weapons by despotic leaders. If women receive such aid, they feed their children, they help their communities, and they bring about a sustainable society. Creative bankers who issue small loans to women to start cottage businesses are among the stories of success proving that women will lead toward a more sustainable society. Education of young girls is an excellent solution to sustaining the future of any country. Two children's corporations are examples of the leadership of mothers. Lil MDGs is a worldwide corporation established in 2005 by a young man from New Hampshire, Dylan Mahalingham. His mother has been his chief supporter as he empowers youth in all corners of the world to end poverty and hunger, providing relief for victims of hurricanes or tsunamis. He discovered that children want to help and get involved. Another corporation, established by Courtney and Eric Honer, two enterprising siblings who were homeschooled by their mother, Jill, is Not So Creepy Critters. They teach about, sell, and in general promote the welfare of spiders, tarantulas, scorpions, and other creepy crawlies. They are leading the way in offering up a new view of our interconnectedness to all life on Earth.

Women comprehend the needs of our planet, and women understand that we want to help and we want to be involved. Women's leadership is developmental, educational, and inspirational. The goal is for the good of this world. Economic, environmental, and social sustainability are naturals for women to come into their own as real leaders.

Seeing Earth from the moon gave us a new image of the fragile nature of our world and the enormous responsibility we have as humans who make conscious choices. We have become an Earth tribe. Three big concepts are in my mind as we go into this decade from 2010 until 2020. *First, we are living longer.* As women, we have enough life left after menopause to allow us to have yet another career. I am living proof of the truth of that statement. *Second*, there is a continual rise of *the power of the feminine* in both males and females. Feminine power is collaborative, communicative, and cooperative. War is not the answer for women. We know too well the advantages of peace at home, peace in our hearts, and peace in the world. Peace begins with one person. It starts in the heart of one being. Women seem to know this. Perhaps our centuries of keeping life foremost in our minds, tending to our homes, our children, and our fellow human beings has equipped us with the possibility of leading toward world peace. Ultimate peace will bring ultimate caring or vice versa. Ultimate caring will bring ultimate peace. The *third* concept is the *connectivity* that is possible through our burgeoning media explosion. Facebook, Twitter, YouTube, cell phones, and the whole Internet were significant factors in the recent Egyptian uprising. More and more we cannot keep secrets from one another.

Women will eventually be aware of the freedom that is their rightful due. These three things—longevity, feminine power, and the hook up through media—are the basis for my belief that women are ready to lead. We do not need to produce all those babies; therefore, we have the time to devote to world tasks. We will eventually receive equal pay for equal work. The statistics as I write this indicate that 80 percent of women in the United States are at parity now. But we also have an evolving consciousness from which women's leadership is emerging.

My favorite mentor, Dr. Jean Houston, says that the feminine principle expresses itself as unfolding of levels of existence, not as a conquest of facts. To the feminine mind, great nature is as important within as it is without; the inward realm has as much status as the external world. We are evolutionally constructed to tend to the inner world; we are ready to make a difference in the sustainability of the earth and all life. Women can lead the people of earth to a sustainable future.

We have a propensity to higher consciousness and greater freedom. We naturally tend to expand. We are quite possibly evolving evolution. Today, this means expansion of ideas through awareness of the connectedness of all life. Global reality and global crisis requires that we look for new thinking to emerge, that we learn from failure and move toward best practices and solutions. What women do you know who serve as examples of this new type of leadership?

I have asked many women to tell me about leadership. I interviewed them to hear stories of leadership. Each of them described leadership as she perceived it. Their responses illustrate something very true for this century. There will be women who are visionary and women who are developers of people. Women will be thought leaders because of their capacity to design, create, imagine, and think. Some will walk ahead, leading the way. Some will partner with others, encouraging and inspiring them to leadership. Some will be like mothers who teach and develop other women or their children, helping them move into their destiny as authentic individual persons. The visionary thought leaders and the people developers will both have conviction of purpose as leaders. Just as mothers have done for centuries, there will be choice of direction based on the good of the whole family, the tribe, the group, and the populace. As Mother Nature does, there will be action that is designed and meant to be conducive to life.

Your Calling

I believe that my work is my calling. That means that I believe in lifelong work since my job is so satisfying and thrilling. I will be happy doing it until I die. Each individual woman can learn about herself and answer the questions, "Who am I?" and "What could I be?" Knowing your talents is the beginning of the answer to those vital questions. Talents are the capacity to do something joyfully. Identifying talents is worth doing. I believe that our strengths are at the heart of motivation. Individual talents, great relationships, positive recognition, and clear expectations work together in the best possible development of us as human beings. Your success will be created from these factors: 1) Your self-concept multiplied by 2) your support system (environment and relationships) and 3) your expectations. These three factors will be divided by the ways in which you manage two other factors—4) your time and 5) your energy. The simple formula for success is Self x Support + Expectations/Time and Energy. To the level all five factors are positive. your success is assured. To the level that any one of them is negative, your success is diminished.

A strengths-based culture will give its people the chance to do what they love to do. When people get to work at something they love and enjoy, they are engaged to the maximum in that work. They show up, they are enthusiastic, they enjoy what they do, and they are healthier. They step up to what is needed.

WORK AS CONTRIBUTION

At InterfaceFLOR, we have been using tools from the Gallup Organization and drawing on the natural talent of each individual. I have had the privilege of serving InterfaceFLOR for more than fifteen years. My own career as a licensed marriage and family therapist prepared me to work in business as a relationship coach. Those people entrusted with leadership at InterfaceFLOR saw fit to allow me to continue to grow that occupation. I don't know anyone today who does exactly what I do, but I have shared with you the written dream in my journal where I conceived of such a job. My hope is that you will do the same. Dream up the career you want. Learn the skills and knowledge it takes to enhance your own talents. Offer up those talents to the world and you will have created the joy of work. From that joy, you will emerge as a leader.

The Age of Emergence

We are moving from an age of power and control into an expanded, advanced age of emergence and creativity. So, we are asking for your answer to the question: "What is the future that wants to emerge?" Women have the capacity to talk about such big ideas. We also are able to create momentum around big ideas. Our style as women is collaborative and informal. Ideas are born when women get together. I remember the women of my farm community coming to our home to sit around the living room, usually to complete a quilt. These sewing circles were the place where ideas were born for the good of our community. Margaret Mead said, "Never doubt that a small group of thoughtful committed citizens can change the world—indeed it is the only thing that ever has." Conversations in an atmosphere of acceptance and safety inspire creativity. Creativity becomes contagious and serves the common good better than guilt or fear.

The coming decades will bring a change in the shape of things to come. Business has traditionally followed a pyramid-shaped management style. Control came from the top of the pyramid, with planning and designing done by very few, who then issued the commands. There has been a shift into management with more participation and inclusion of many minds in designing processes and making decisions. With women moving into leadership, the predictions are that management styles will continue to morph into flatter organizational structure based on more input from everyone involved. The shape is less pyramidal and more circular. One vice president told me recently that the circle style has relieved him of being responsible for all the decisions and that he likes the more collaborative style. I am an advocate of the circle way with a leader in every chair. The structure is circular—a round table—where all are equal and welcome. Yes, that makes King Arthur the first Possible Woman-aware leader. The only difference was he lacked female knights. The Possible Woman stepping up represents female knights of the round table! And it is an Aquarian Age table.

MAGIC CIRCLE

Years ago, I did my dissertation on a subject that no one had studied before. I called it "Linguistic Emotion," suggesting that emotions are fixed in the language of origin. In order to examine this idea, I used a method called "Magic Circle," an affective curriculum created by Uvaldo Palomares and Geraldine Ball. I learned how to train teachers in the use of Magic Circle, and we created an experiment where selected elementary school children were offered Magic Circle in Spanish, their language of origin. Others received Magic Circle in English. The only thing I proved in the yearlong study was that the children who loved school, liked their teacher, and were happy were the ones who experienced Magic Circle in their native language. These circles of children are images in my mind that illustrate true engagement. Their bright eyes and eager minds told me that something magical was happening in every circle. My study gained me approval of the dissertation, and I was awarded the degree. The circle way was embedded in my thinking as a means for inclusion and engagement (presence) of everyone present. Every child in the classroom was able to express freely. I carried that method into my work with offices, businesses, and corporate meetings. We would sit in circles where everyone was invited to talk. An atmosphere of inclusion and acceptance was part of the design. There is something to be said for an experience designed in such a way that individuals feel secure enough that they can talk, they can listen, they will be heard, and there will be no put-downs. The rules of Magic Circle were simple, and it turns out that the same kind of circle meeting really can be beneficial in a business setting.

Women are accustomed to working in flat organizations. From the earliest sewing bees, to quilting circles, to knitting circles, to family meals around a table, women know how to collaborate. Collaborative creativity is the wave of the future. Cubicle offices are not as popular as informal "nested" offices in the changing world of creative business. Our world of work is adapting to the styles that women have used forever. I believe that Mother Nature knows best. Whatever project your work demands, Mother Nature has the model to follow.

Mother Nature: The Mother Lode

Mother Nature provides a tried and proven path to conceive, develop, manage, and complete any project. She is the Mother Lode, the mentor, the model, and the measure for project management success. Success is possible in any project design if nature's model is studied and applied. We have only to mine this rich vein of wisdom.

I learned a lot about integrating Mother Nature into the world of work when I met Dr. Janine Benyus and Dr. Dayna Baumeister. *Biomimicry,* as described by Janine Benyus in her book by the same name, helps us to study and imitate the natural way of doing things. When deciding how to pursue a project, the key is to ask, "How would nature do this task"? Mother Nature really does know best.

Nature's cycles are designed for survival. Our human species is nearing the crisis of survival due to consumption of nature's bounty without regard for the whole system. We human beings are beginning to "get it"; we realize we are one with nature, and we exist in living systems.

A new natural science of the human being might include all the previous science fields (biology, psychology, ecology, sociology, theology, etc.). I heard Margaret Meade, the great anthropologist, speaking at Rice University in Houston, Texas, in the 1970s. Margaret said that we need a new science of the human being. She suggested it could include all of the "ologies." And we will then come together to solve our human problems. We can learn to coexist with nature. The addition of biology to the field of study of humans is interesting and intriguing. I hope we will wake up enough to understand and use principles of natural development before we completely foul our nest.

My work is my contribution to my world. I offer it with humility, risking that it will be received in such a way that the good of our world is moved upward and outward, expanding human potential. Do you work to live or do you live to work? The women who seem most engaged and most fulfilled enjoy their work. Others tell me that they work only for the money it brings them. These are the people who gave up on any kind of soul satisfaction that comes from pursuit of individual passion. Passion appears when we are working on the path of fulfillment of our life purpose. Our talents serve our life purpose. Our best productivity comes when we are aligned with our strengths. Work is at its best when we do what we enjoy doing. Energy, engagement, and successful productivity are the side effects of working at what we really love to do.

I chose business as my first college course of study. The constraints felt by women born before WWII in the first half of the twentieth century were limitations in our choice of work. When women were invited to serve as part of the defense movement, enabling the war to be won, we crossed a threshold that meant the limits were surpassed. In the middle of this past century, women were released to join the workforce. Two-income families became the norm, and marriage also was transformed. Divorce became a common solution to relationship discord because a woman could make a living, supporting her family on one income plus child support from the ex-spouse. The shift toward independence has been world-changing. At the time I am writing this, there is a 52 percent rate of divorce for first marriages, and it escalates for each succeeding marriage. We live in changing times. You are a woman who will create the future through your individual beliefs, thoughts, feelings, and behaviors. Your career is your contribution. Your work can also be your calling.

Do you really want to become a leader? Are you beginning to want to be fully engaged in all of your life? All of your life includes your professional self, your physical self, your personal self, as well as your passion. Knowing your purpose in life means knowing what thrills you, what draws you, and what magnetizes you forward into unknown realms of leadership. My own life's purpose has been defined through trial and error. Effective psychotherapy helped me to know who I am and where I want to go. Finding my passion for certain activities helped me, knowing the north node of the moon in my natal chart helped me, and discovering what I was really good at doing helped me. It is not too surprising that I am in the career that also is my purpose in life. It has also provided the most life satisfaction. I wake up every day full of anticipation for the unfolding of my purpose as it presents itself through daily activities, appointments, and interactions.

Leadership means to me that I am, first, the leader of myself. After that, I simply do what I really want to do, and it turns out, that is my life job. My hope for you is that you find your calling and that you are able to make your unique and significant contribution through the joy of your work.

Strengths

How do I know that I am in the flow of using my unique talents? What evidence do I have that tells me I am on track, coming from my optimum self-development?

First, I have a state of concentration, and I am focused on what I am doing. Second, I have a feeling of satisfaction or absorption in whatever I am doing. Third, my feelings are positive. One of the best indicators that I am off track is that I have gathered up negative feelings. When there is a cloud of darkness, doubt, or irritation, I can be certain that I am not operating from strengths.

Fourth, I am in the mindset of possibilities—not feeling constrained or fearful. It is like using my brain to pursue some mystery or curiosity with the same avid dedication as a dog sniffing some trail and chasing some quarry. These possibilities are exciting and challenging at the same time. It is like working a puzzle and not wanting to stop until I have solved it.

These are autotelic experiences, meaning that they come from within me. They are the true me, operating from my own autonomy. I find it amusing that I will doggedly pursue some task if I am the one deciding to do the task. I have less interest in pursuing a task assigned from the outside by someone else. If the outside task is interesting and I have mastery of how to do it, there is a better chance I will do it with enthusiasm. Getting to do what I do best is inextricably linked with my positive emotions. Strengths seem to flourish when autonomy is guaranteed. I am able to perform tasks when I have mastery over that performance. And if the task seems to have a valid purpose, I will enter it with great intention to perform well.

Motivation is linked to autonomy, mastery, and purpose. Daniel Pink has demonstrated this in his book *Drive*. Autonomy was established in the toddler stage of your life when you were learning to walk and talk. Your outside caretakers were involved in helping you conform to the standards of the day by their toilet training. Autonomy means being in charge of your body. Purpose is revealed at play age, when you were four or five years old. You began to make ideas and have creative thoughts, and you took your intentions into action. Mastery is adding skills to your repertoire. We start school and begin to master the art of reading, writing, and arithmetic, so the earliest development of your drive or your motivation came before you were a teenager. Awareness of your life and the stories you tell about your past will help you understand yourself in present-day activities. Leadership is rooted in autonomy (self-starting); purpose (ideas and intention); and mastery (skills and knowledge).

Leadership in Real Life

Your leadership in real life may be in different settings. You can be a leader in your home, community, volunteer organizations, church, schools, hospitals, politics, philosophy, or anywhere you find yourself every day. Leading means to be present. Leading means to know your Self. Leading means to know your talents. Leading means to offer up your gifts and talents for the greater good of your world. You are the Possible Woman, ready to bring about meaningful change—beneficial change—for the good of all life on this incredible planet, where we live and have our being. The time has come for you to step up.

Leading a Circle Meeting

One of the best skills you can learn is how to conduct a meeting. There are many disciplines that you can study. I offer one that has served well in my world—leading by collaboration. I found that the best way to hold a collaborative meeting is to meet in a circle. The best way to encourage collaboration is to create an atmosphere where each person is a leader. A leader in every chair sets the pattern for all ideas to be welcome. The tone of the meeting is built upon inclusivity that welcomes diversity. Ideas are welcome, judgment is deferred, and all brains are acceptable. I offer a sample of such a circle meeting. Use it, build upon it, improve it, and make it your own. My wish and my suggestion is that you create your own version of Magic Circle.

If you are the facilitator for a meeting, the following are guidelines that I recommend you follow.

Background questions to be answered and understood before the meeting:

1. What are we doing?
2. Why are we doing it?
3. What is the desired outcome?

You, as facilitator, will be in charge of hospitality and welcome. You are responsible for making sure the members of the group have received timely communication regarding where, when, and why you are meeting. You are the one who makes sure that the group is comfortably seated in a circle, that you start and stop on time, and that the goal for the meeting is met for the best possible outcome.

If ideas are being solicited, large groups will need to be subdivided. These small groups should be no more than five to fifteen people, with a leader-facilitator chosen by the group after they are formed. These small groups will be charged with specific action items in a time frame clearly stated, with outcomes cleared explained.

When the circle is convened, your job as leader is to state the topic for this session and review the guidelines for the meeting. You can create your own guidelines. These are the ones I like:

1. Everyone gets to talk
2. Everyone is listened to with attention and respect
3. No putdowns, no bucket-dipping

4. Solutions invited, creativity encouraged, brainstorming allowed
5. Stay on the topic for this session
6. Honor the time allotment
7. Where have we been and where are we going?
8. What is the future that wants to emerge?

We have an example from the past. The Iroquois nation brought peace among warring tribes through such a meeting of leaders. They sat in a circle where each was given time to talk and the others listened respectfully (Benjamin Franklin reported how remarkable was their deep listening: "Not at all like the British House of Commons where everyone shouts and interrupts."). At the end of the meeting of the tribal council, they had found new solutions, which brought them to their objective—peaceful coexistence.

In this circle, all are included, and all are valued. The takeaway will be known only after we have offered our ideas. The solutions are heretofore unknown and undefined. This is emergent phenomenon, and it will, by definition, be creative. Our takeaways will be what we have generated in these few hours of our time together in dialogue. Each speaker will present ideas and best practices. Each will challenge you, the listeners, with questions. These questions will stimulate our design iterations.

Your Power

In past centuries, power has traditionally been of two kinds: masculine power, which is more about command and control, rationally created from brain function (head), or feminine power, which is more about feelings and yearnings, emotionally created from the heart. Both males and females have the power to bring forth qualities of creativity, self-expression, love, intimacy, spiritual matters, talent development, and a better future for our world. We can establish societies that value cooperation, communion, and connectedness aimed at our essential human flourishing. Instead of living out a competitive individualism, we can "get it" that we are a collective, powerful force, with consciousness as our evolutionary growth mechanism. Our real power as men and as women lies in our minds. The taming of the mind through creative consciousness is where real power lies. Awareness of our thoughts, feelings, behavior patterns, and ownership of the world we create through our projections is power in action. The power is spiritual, mental, and physical. We are all in this life together; we are both separate and one; and we can join in creating a future that does want to emerge. The partnership way of co-creation can bring forth feminine power as well as masculine strength.

Conclusion

I am writing this in 2011. My life on this planet (this lifetime) began in 1929. I lived the first fifteen years of my life in a house with a coal stove for heating, a kerosene cook stove, an outdoor toilet, water drawn by a windmill from a well that I watched being drilled, no telephone, a battery-powered radio that received two or three stations, a wind-charger that kept the battery charged, a barn with cows that were milked and fed every day, chickens that gave us their eggs and were butchered for their meat, gardens and truck patches, apricot and apple trees, and sandstorms. I hoed cotton, I drove the tractor while they headed maize, and I turned the DeLaval cream separator. I was a farm hand. I learned everything I could find to learn. I read every book I could get. I was quick and good at math, and I could read very well. I never thought about being a person who could lead. I dreamed about houses that had electricity and an education that would get me a job that paid money. I could buy clothes with the money. I chose to major in business so I could get a job. My consciousness did not really begin to wake up and grow up until I was widowed at age thirty-three. I was not prepared to lead my family. To this day, I ask forgiveness from my children for my inadequacy as their mother in that time of family fracture. I knew I had to work or else my family could not live.

The career path I took was to become a counselor, which required that I get my own counseling. From those years of examining my own life, my consciousness began to expand, and I matured. That process is continuing today. Over the past forty years, I have had the real privilege of "sitting in the chair" and listening to the stories of thousands of people. The majority of those people were women. I came to know the psyche of women. I have observed the generational shifts as we change in our culture. I have watched the strictness of pre-World War II morals as they have come to a world of individuality, creative expression, and personal freedom. Women seem to survive. Women seem to thrive under the worst of circumstances. Women endure. As Ashley Montague wrote in his book *The Natural Superiority of Women*, women are tougher, stronger, withstand stress better, live longer, and are superior in every aspect except physical prowess.

Our talents as women are born of two to five thousand years of being relegated to the second sex—second-class citizens. That is no longer true. We are capable, we can work, and we can lead. At least this is true in our country. We are educated, and we can create. We can envision the future, and we can develop the people who will create that future.

You are ready to lead. Your leadership is vitally necessary now that we are entering the Aquarian Age. You are the real and true Possible Woman, ready to step up. Stepping up to the life of the planet Earth means restoring the physical environment, creating social sustainability, and revitalizing the economic health of our commerce. These are the ways in which women will lead us into meaningful change. You can do it. The world needs you. I am so happy to see you stepping into your rights and your responsibilities as leaders. Who knows what the future will be when we are equal in power as well as responsibility? I know that you, the women of tomorrow, are capable of creating a future that wants to emerge.

Afterword

In addition to my work as a relationship and strengths coach for InterfaceFLOR, I have worked this year on a side project that included writing this book. I took the job of getting the manuscript into full form. Getting up early in the mornings to write has really helped. Staying focused has helped. Knowing why I am doing this work helps. All of that desire to make a difference and to encourage women to see themselves as leaders in our time gives me motivation to write, even though I am not trained, nor do I perceive myself to be a writer. I am an author, maybe, of ideas and concepts but not a proficiently skilled writer. Our self-doubts can stop us from pursuing out-of-the-box thinking as well as dampening our daydreams.

As I pursue this project by writing this book, I meet myself in negative, self-downing thoughts. When that happens, I deliberately shift my thinking, returning to the positive path. My desire is to envision this next dream as fully as possible, seeing it being helpful to both women and men. My imagination includes seeing them asking me to speak about the concepts in the book, imagining full court press in distributing it. When I dream preposterously, I see it catching on with public acceptance, media coverage, and more exposure, allowing the abundance to spread the words I am writing. That inspires me to make the words full of punch and meaning and to imagine my book touching the hearts and minds of women, inspiring them to fully accept themselves, grow their talents, and assume their rightful roles as leaders in today's world. I dream about women playing their music, singing their songs in the dance of life, speaking their words, and feeling their friendliness with joyful anticipation of an evolved, emerging future. I want to encourage, inspire, and evoke women's development to the fullest, highest possible level.

About the Author

Marj Barlow was a marriage and family therapist for 30 years before she became a consultant to business and industry. Since 1996, she has worked with InterfaceFLOR as a relationship coach and strengths coach. Another endeavor has been her dedication to women's leadership development. The Possible Woman was her concept that has grown into a broad program for women, led by Linda Wind of Wind Enterprises®. Her first book, *The Possible Woman*, was published in 1998 for use on Possible Woman cruises and seminars. She also published a book for couples use, *Couples Night Out* in 1988.

She was born in Ralls, TX in 1929. Her education includes degrees in business, psychology, and education. She has lived in Canyon, Kingsville, Corpus Christi, Austin, TX and Lincoln, NE.

Marj lives in Buda, TX with her husband Paul. They have five adult children, three grandchildren and three great grandchildren. They enjoy being called, "GeeGee and Gampa." The sign at their front door says, "Beginner's Heaven" and the signs on their back porch read, "Live, Love, Laugh, Look, Listen, Learn, Liberate, and Leave a Legacy.

Made in the USA
Lexington, KY
09 April 2019